[illegible signature], 2012

ISLAND

"paint the light within"

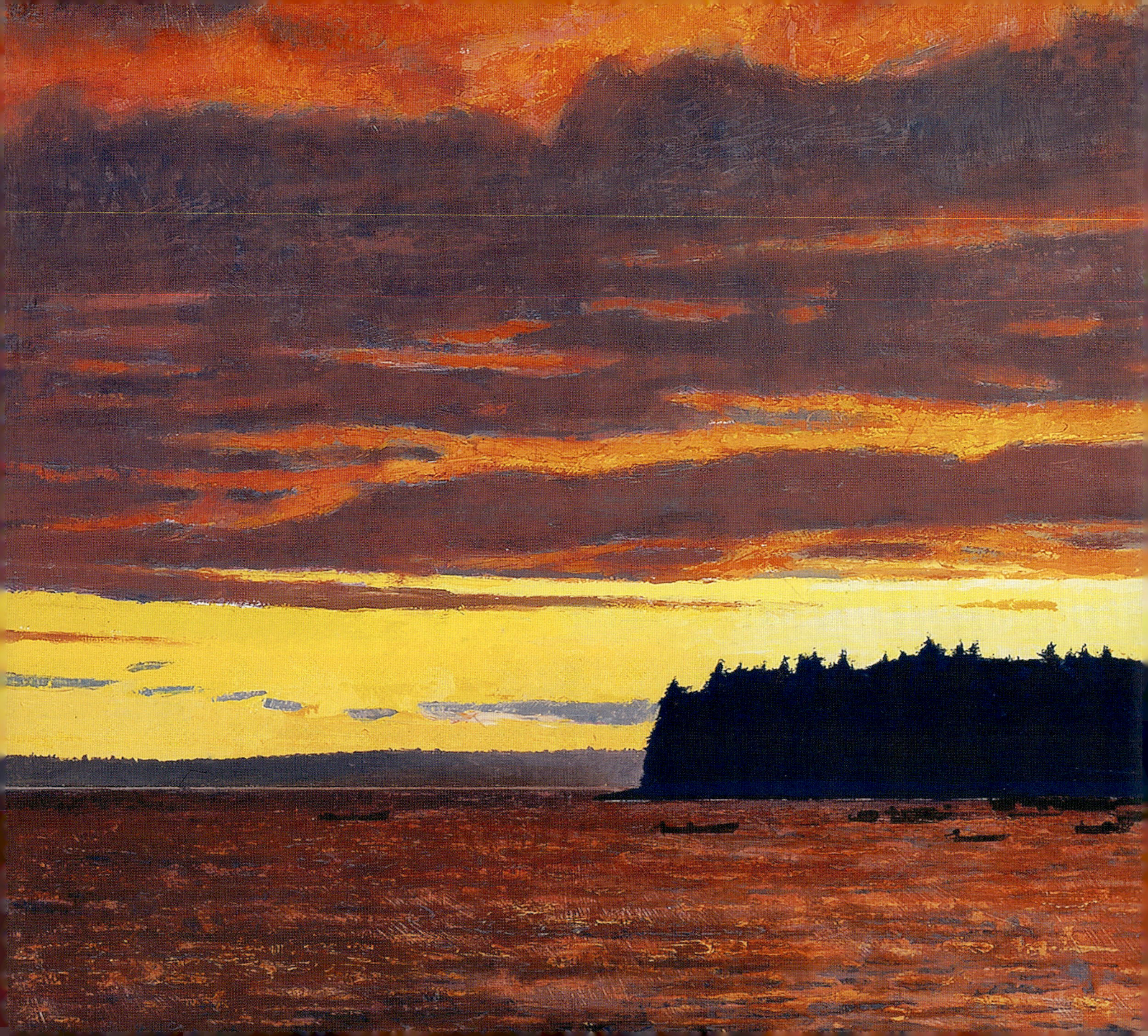

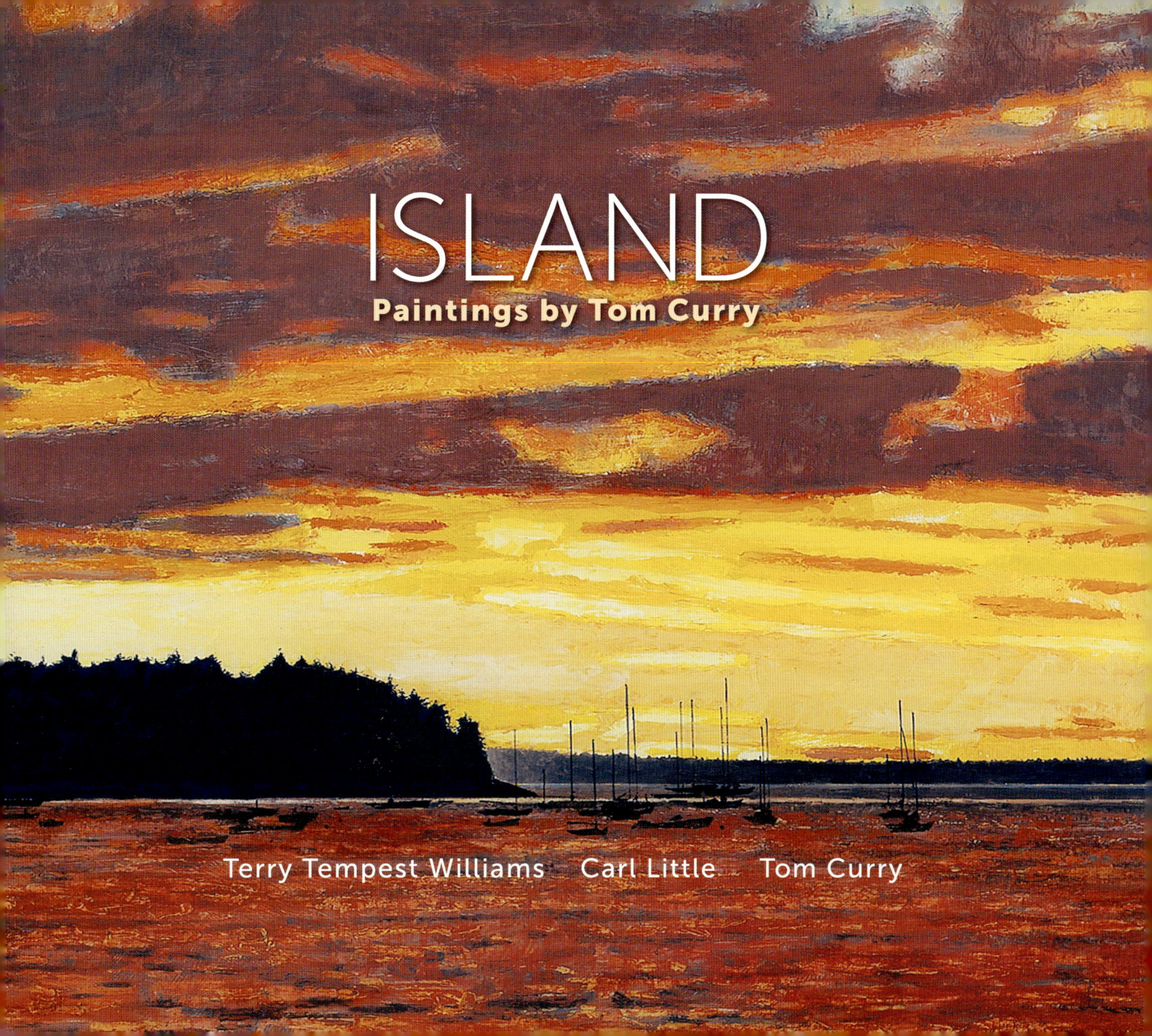

ISLAND

Paintings by Tom Curry

Terry Tempest Williams   Carl Little   Tom Curry

This book originated from a larger, unpublished work developed and packaged by Academy Press and Jan Cigliano Hartman

ISBN: 978-1-60893-003-6

Design by Lynda Chilton

Printed in China
5 4 3 2 1

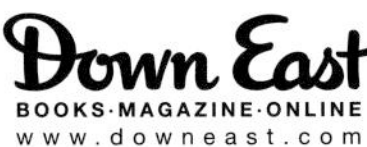

Distributed to the trade by National Book Network

Library of Congress Cataloging-in-Publication Data

Williams, Terry Tempest.
Island : paintings by Tom Curry / Terry Tempest Williams, Carl Little, Tom Curry.
p. cm.
"Adapted from a larger unpublished work developed and packaged by Academy Press and Jan Cigliano Hartman."
ISBN 978-1-60893-003-6 (trade hardcover : alk. paper)
1. Curry, Tom (Tom J.), 1957—Themes, motives. 2. Islands in art. I. Curry, Tom (Tom J.), 1957- II. Little, Carl. III. Title. IV. Title: Paintings by Tom Curry.
ND237.C882W55 2012
759.13–dc23

2011043503

Dusk, pastel on paper, 25" x 31", private collection.

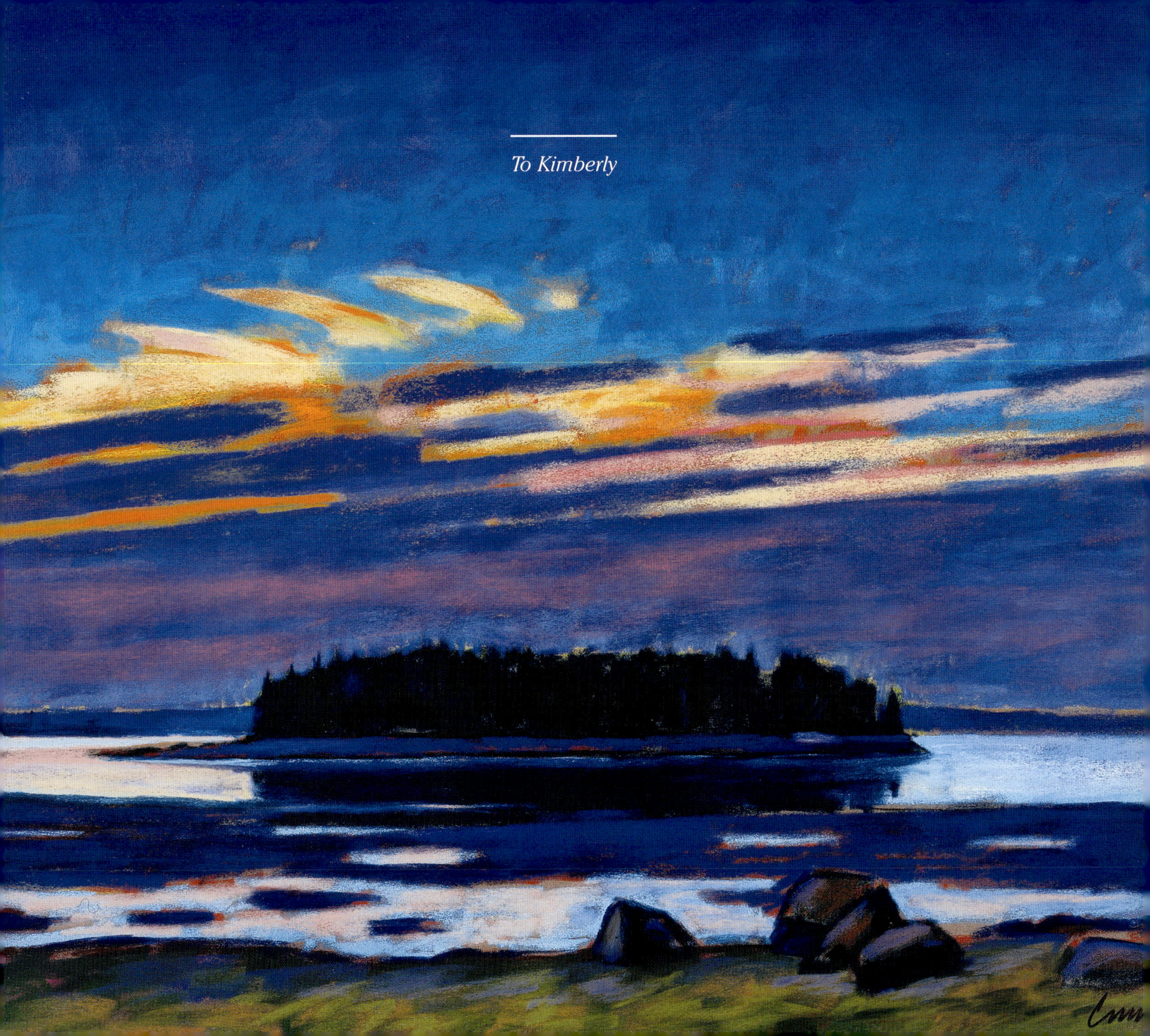

To Kimberly

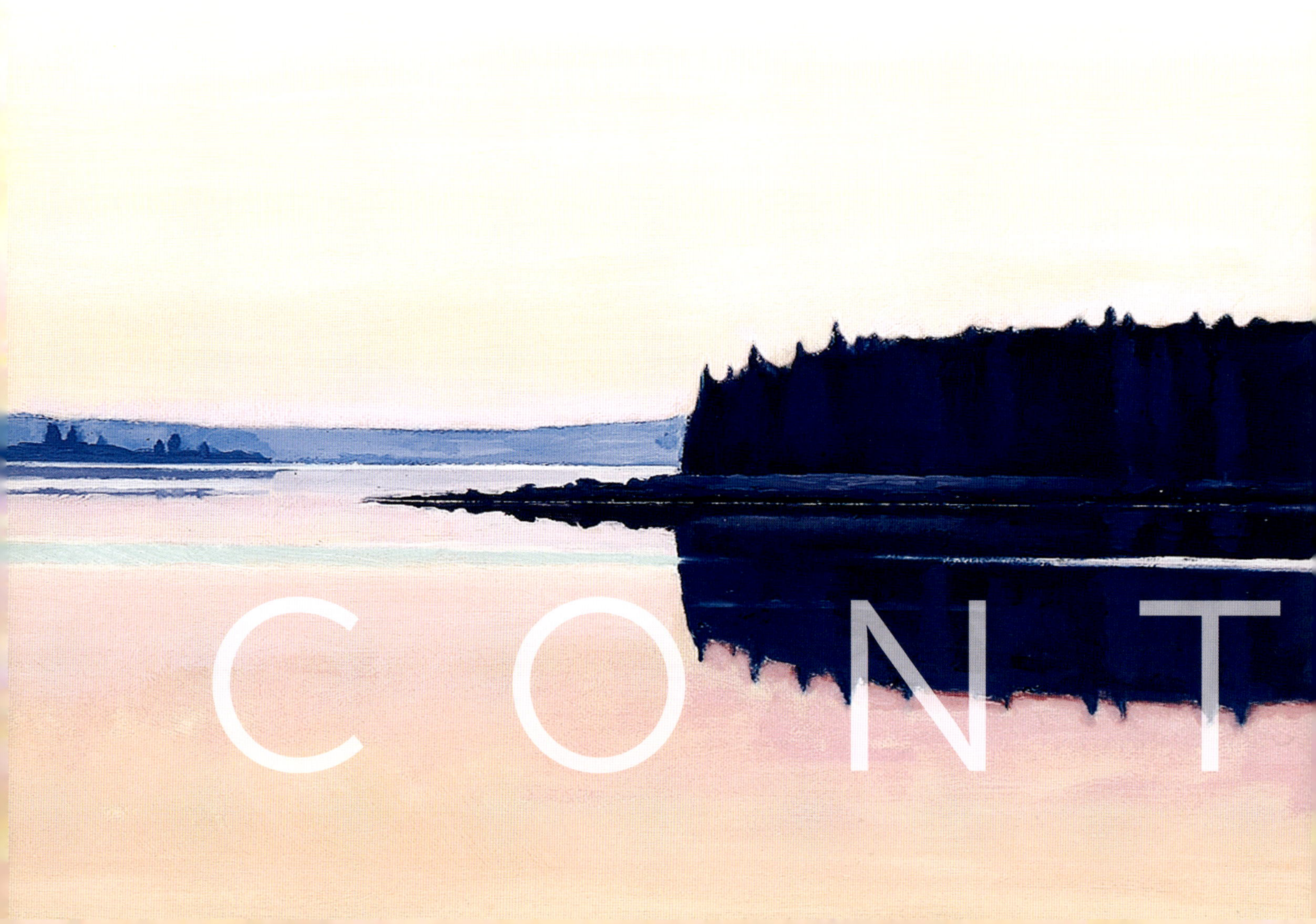
C O N T

ENTS

"The light moves so fast—how can I ever hold onto anything?"

—Tom Curry

Morning After the Storm, oil on panel, 36" x 43", collection of John Randall.

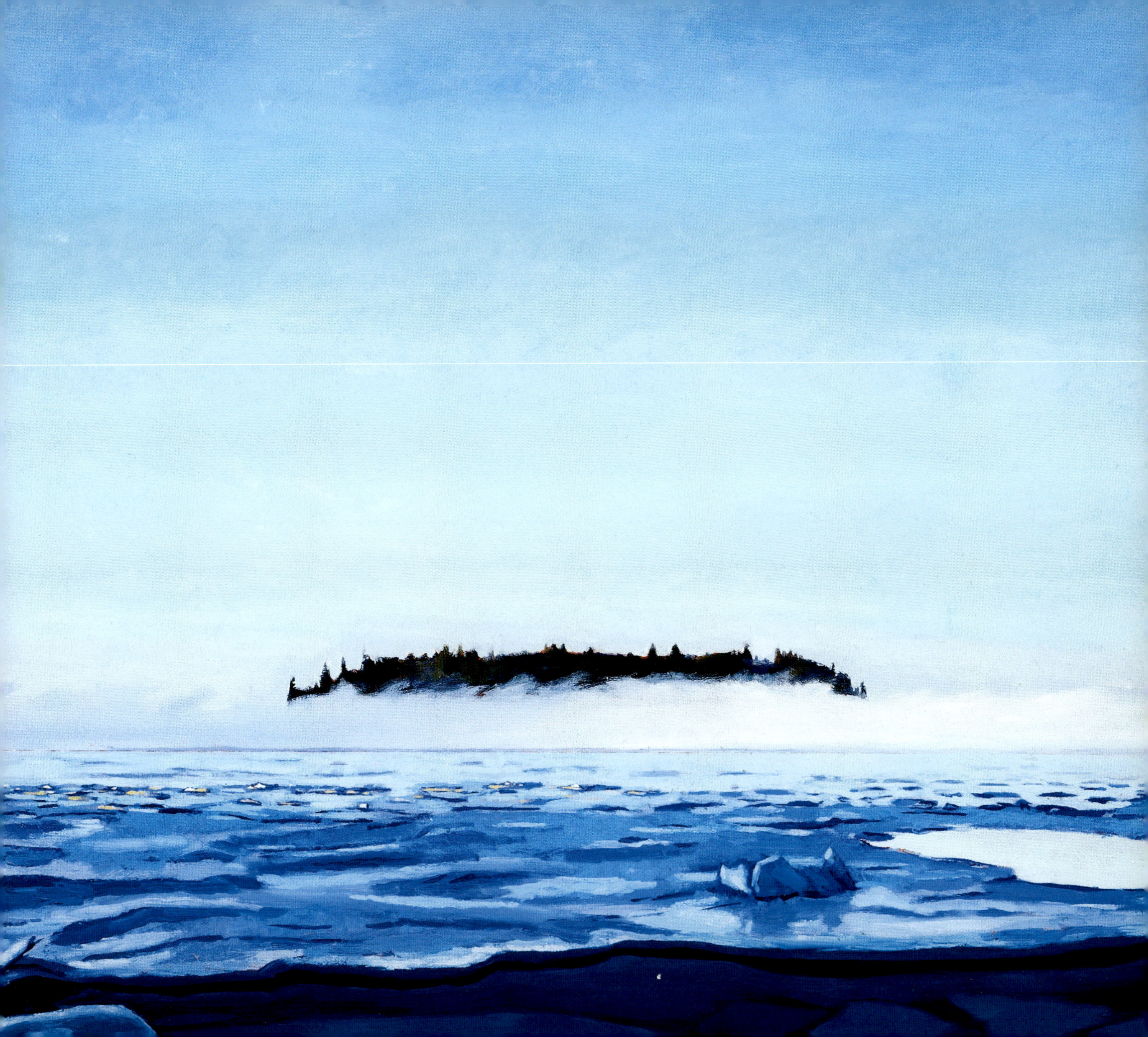

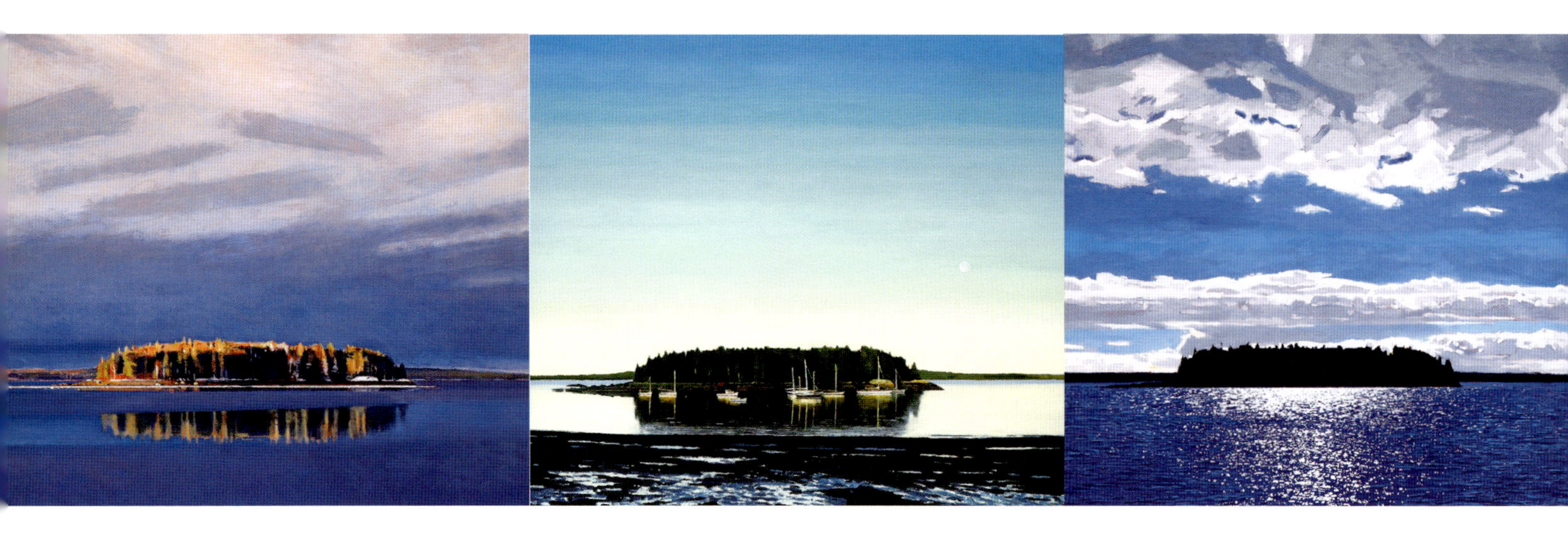

The Animation of Spirit:

Painting the Invisible

Terry Tempest Williams

Every summer and fall I migrate to Maine, where the daily breathing of tides becomes the mantra of the sea's edge. It is here I return like the least sandpiper to probe the wrack line for sustenance. It is here I have come to rely on the abundance of salt marshes and the braiding of eelgrass to untangle my mind. And it is here I have learned that when the crows gather in the arms of balsam firs and birches, crying incessantly, a bald eagle is near.

It is also here where I met Tom Curry, a landscape painter who lives on the Blue Hill Peninsula. "How do you paint Spirit?" I once asked him. He didn't answer. It is not a question I have asked myself as a writer.

A few years later, I found myself inside Tom's studio looking at new paintings. I witnessed light dancing on water. Paint on canvas awakened the ineffable, and my longing, whose source eludes me, returned.

Agitation is not often paired with contemplation, but I believe these words are siblings. A restlessness precedes or prompts the cry for reflection. The mental tossing we experience as crashing waves within the walls of our mind begs for the pause of tranquility. How else will we find our way in a world as discursive and distractive as ours?

“The only wisdom we can hope to acquire,” wrote T. S. Eliot, “is the wisdom of humility.” I think of Maine’s rocky coast. Acadia. Monhegan. Surf crashing, plumes of sea smoke rising, the sloshing of water back and forth in the confines of a granite trough. It is the oscillations between thrust and pause, emptiness and explosion that keep us in the dynamic stance of watchfulness as we contemplate the nature of relentless power.

One night, I floated on my back in Morgan Bay, the ocean waters of Surry, Maine, with my arms outstretched like a cross. I was cradled in water, rocked back and forth by the sea, as the Milky Way bathed me in starlight. In that moment, I felt blessed, and dissolved.

Curry’s Chatto Island paintings are a meditation. His close perusal of water, the undulating ripples between shadow and light that occur in moments of calm and disturbance, brings us into the emotional relief of memory. We know that island.

We have witnessed that moment. On one day, Curry’s brushstrokes create a skiff of ice and a reflection melting from the last rays of daylight. On another day, he paints the dazzling dance of water as the island sleeps.

We do not look at these paintings so much as feel them like a heat wave in August. They are the visceral expressions of all the various moods we experience living on the edge of water.

In my favorite island meditation, it is snowing. “An immense whispering” is heard. Each flake is painted as a world falling. The foreground is transparent, blue green, sheets of ice are exposed beneath the opaque water. Ice slabs crack and break the chilled serenity. The island rests like a great stillness upon the sea, housing secrets that will be kept until summer.

What is an island but a body? The human body awakens. We emerge from the seas upright, cellular bodies with legs and arms and eyes that blink to register the clarity of forms known and unknown, the result of joyous struggle and experimentation.

I don't know what keeps the artist returning to his easel day after day, or the writer to her desk, when despair creeps in and threatens to quell the imagination, the source of our deepest hope as human beings. To evoke what we can never say, to honor what we can never know, and to illuminate what we can only feel, is the truest rendering of our soul's work.

Tom Curry follows the animation of spirit. What is invisible becomes the secret muscle that calls forth tides and keeps them rushing forward, fingers of foam on the reach. But it is in the retreat that treasures are found: a shell, a stone, a buoy unmoored from a fisherman's boat, now an artifact. This is the wisdom of return that the ocean knows and we seek each time we walk to the water's edge and follow the wrack line.

The return. Curry's gift to us is always the return, the return to the island. The return of light on the water. The return of the seasonal palette before him. His courage as an artist is his belief in the holy act of repetition and return. The island he paints over and over again is a shimmering liturgy of light, transcendent.

"The face of the sea is always changing, crossed by colors, lights and moving shadows, sparkling in the sun, mysterious in the twilight, its aspects and its moods vary hour by hour."

—Rachel Carson, from *The Sea Around Us*

Sea Smoke, oil on panel, 36" x 43", collection of Nancy and Bucky Kales.

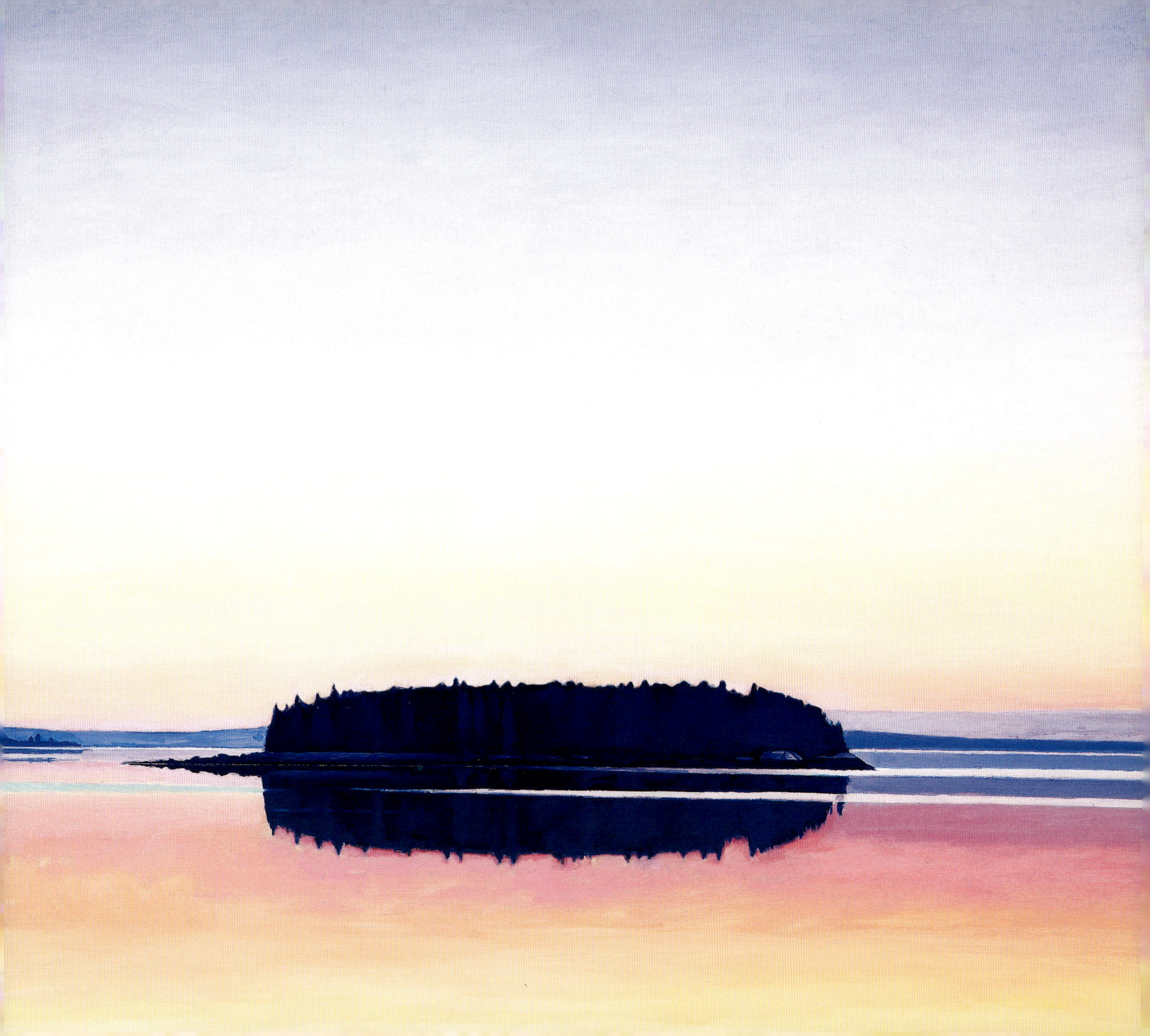

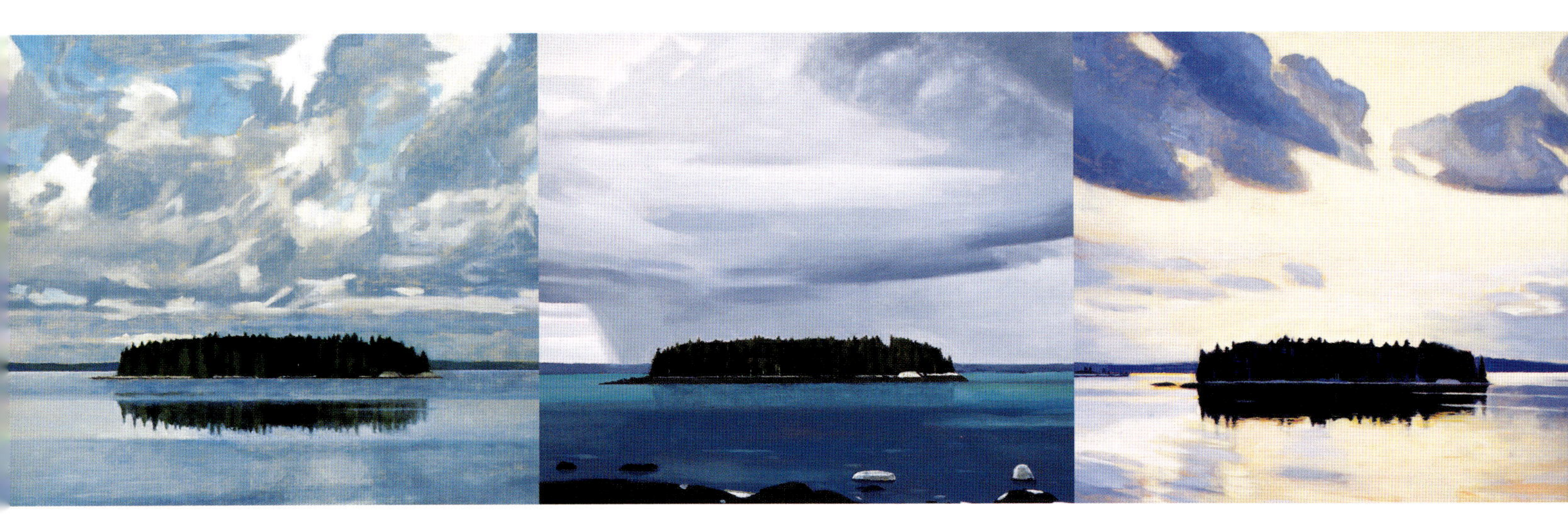

Coming to Light:

The Maine Islands of Tom Curry

Carl Little

The history of American art offers a variety of islands, from Childe Hassam's Appledore in the Isles of Shoals to Walter Anderson's Horn Island off the coast of Mississippi. In these and other cases, the artist brought a level of obsession to the subject, which led to paintings that have the authenticity of a place experienced.

With its impressive archipelago, Maine is well represented in this rich thematic line. Monhegan Island alone has inspired a distinguished roster of some of America's finest landscape painters, from George Bellows and Edward Hopper to Reuben Tam and Jamie Wyeth.

Artists often become intimately associated with a particular Maine island—Fairfield Porter and Great Spruce Head, William Kienbusch and Hurricane Island, Carolyn Brady and Vinalhaven, or Bo Bartlett and Matinicus. The island becomes a nurturing place, a retreat and refuge, a source of art and energy.

The spruce-clad isles along the coast have beckoned Tom Curry since he and his wife, writer Kimberly Ridley, moved to the state in 1995. One island in particular has held him captive: humble and handsome Chatto.

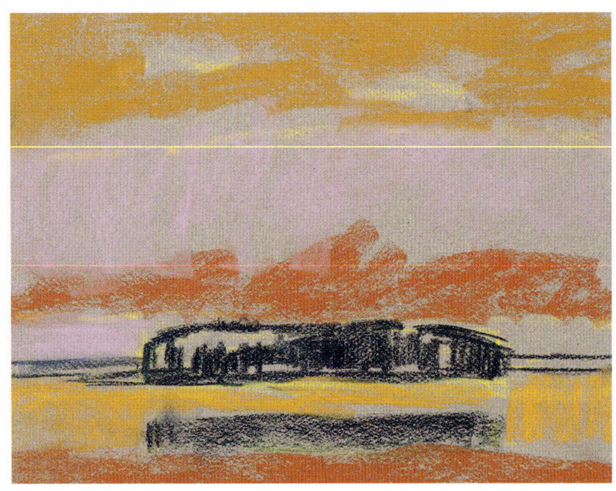

Island Study, pastel on paper, 10" x 13", collection of the artist.

Curry's first representation of Chatto Island, which sits just off Center Harbor in the village of Brooklin, on the Blue Hill Peninsula, was a pastel drawn in 1996. That striking depiction of a dark island under a sun-pierced evening sky was the touchstone. In the years that followed, Curry found himself attached to Chatto.

In the pastel, he established the composition—a template, as it were—for subsequent renderings. The island sits low on the horizon, mediating, as it were, between sky and water. Its roughly rectangular shape, equidistant from the right and left edges of the canvas, breaks up the horizon. Around this central shape the elements change: clouds build up, sailboats come and go, a sliver of distant Deer Isle coastline emerges or recedes according to the day.

The Chatto paintings are not the traditional dramatic islandscape, in which the viewer encounters waves crashing over ledges, a bold headland, a dramatic sweep of coastline. The island is often modest, almost Zen-like—a simple point of attention that nonetheless taps into a deep-seated connection. It floats in the near distance: an island to hold at arm's length, like a treasured object.

Curry describes Chatto as the "top of a mountain; everything is happening underneath and around it." The island is the most stationary entity in a constantly shifting landscape: rising and receding tides, a sky in flux, fog and sea smoke curtaining the view. Nothing stays the same except for the island, although its shape changes, too: one day a silhouette, another, a phantom presence. "And sometimes it's gone," notes the artist.

Over the years, Curry has painted more than forty "portraits" of Chatto Island. It is a motif, but also a point of physical and spiritual reference.

A Realism Based on Felt Experience

Each Chatto painting offers a harmony of color. Several winter pieces are tonal studies in pale whites and grays. Against this all-of-a-piece palette, Curry often mixes the treatment: a painterly foreground and a refined sky may share the same canvas. Many paintings contrast a dark foreground with a bright sky, while in others the sea and sky are connected by reflection.

The Chatto paintings sometime recall the landscapes of Ferdinand Hodler, who Curry has acknowledged as a significant influence. He shares the Swiss painter's pursuit of the sublime—that sense of awe felt in the encounter with an Alp or an island—as well as his obsession with certain landscape motifs.

Whether a pale wash of pure light or the setting for a configuration of clouds, Curry's skies elicit a sense of wonder. From painting to painting the eye is engaged by backlit clouds or seamless spectra of color. Whatever the lineaments of the view may be—the lighting conditions, the weather or season, the specific assembly of clouds—the painter is always wondering how close he can get the painting to conveying what he is experiencing. His is a realism based on felt experience.

In this regard, one thinks of Rockwell Kent. Moving from New York City to remote Monhegan Island in 1904, Kent embraced the place as an artist and individual. The paintings he created as a year-round islander stand as his most genuine—experienced, not transcribed. Curry's Chatto paintings convey that same earned truth.

At the same time, Curry's island has a mythical aspect. The paintings are more than simply portraits of an island. Often dark, sometimes shrouded or eerily doubled by its reflection in the sea, Chatto can be guardian or ghost.

"The light moves so fast—how can I ever hold onto anything?" Curry asks himself. He maintains a kind of diary of the island, recording impressions—studies, mostly sketches, and small pastels, made on site, plus 35mm slides. Yet for all the preparation involved in setting up to paint the island, Curry relies primarily on memory. "I don't have to be looking at the island; I absolutely know it," he states.

Among the most remarkable qualities of the Chatto series is the freshness of each new portrayal. Where you might think that spark of engagement in treating the same motif every year might diminish, the painter maintains the kind of innocent vision that originally called him to Chatto. In this regard, Curry is like the Chinese painters and poets from ancient times responding to the same mountain, each time looking for and finding new depths of understanding.

Reverence for Place: Painting the Maine Landscape

In Maine, Curry has learned to appreciate orientation. From an urban milieu where he rarely saw the stars, where he moved through manmade grids with little physical reference, the painter suddenly wanted to know where north was. He quickly recognized that an awareness of his coordinates was tied to survival. He admired how fishermen knew the daily tides, appreciated shifts in the wind, and could read weather signs.

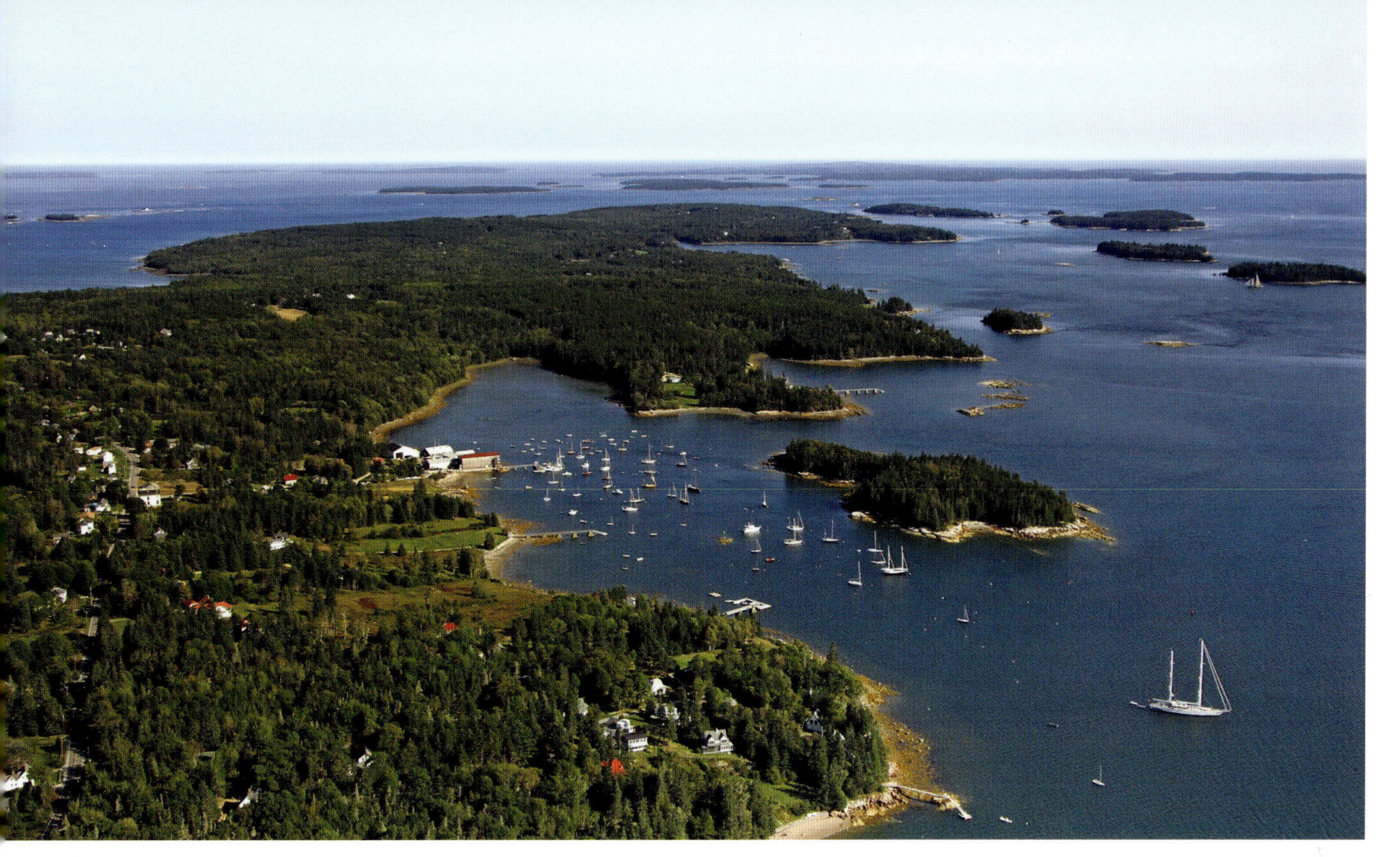

Aerial view of Chatto Island. (GMW Holdings LLC)

"The five-day forecast is the way suburbia takes care of nature," Curry states. His tack changed in Maine. In conversations with Sedgwick painter Chris Baker, he came to understand the importance of directly experiencing his surroundings. "Spend at least two hours each day outside all year," Baker told him. Immersion would lead to authentic vision.

The painter has a number of revelatory stories related to the landscape. In one, he is cross-country skiing with a friend and looking at the shoreline in the fog. Without a camera or a sketchbook to record the impression, he makes a visual note: fantastic green color. The impression stays in his head till he manages to put something down in paint.

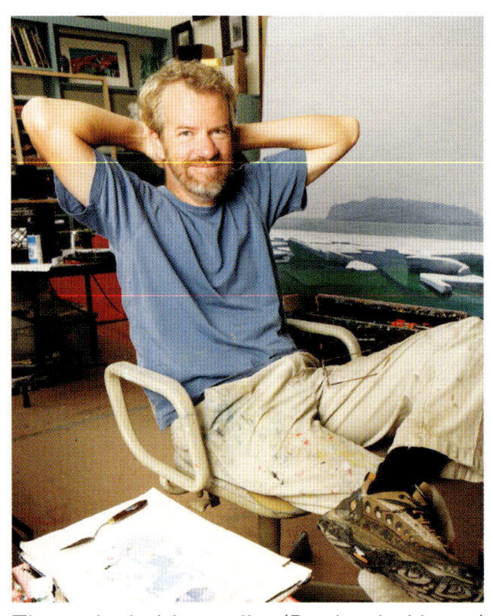
The artist in his studio. (Benjamin Magro)

Another story relates to driving his wife to the Searsport bus station at five in the morning and seeing "this light glare off the water in a particular manner." The vision was so beautiful it made his hair stand on end. Again Curry made a mental record. That particular effect, he vowed, would "work its way into something."

Curry likens himself to the wanderer in the desert looking for a sign—the burning bush. In his Maine world, an island appears and disappears in the sea; seasons arrive with their individual palettes; light beguiles. As he seeks an essence and a mystery in his northern surroundings, Curry remains a student of nature.

Inside the Studio

In Curry's studio in Brooklin, Maine, on a cold bright January morning, the aroma of painting supplies accents the air and light streams through broad windows, illuminating the warm space. The studio, which Curry has occupied since 1996, was once the second-floor gym of the Brooklin School, which served kindergarten through 8th-grade students from this small boat-building town.

Along one wall of the studio run shelving and cases holding art supplies and a substantial library. The latter is a wonderfully eclectic assortment, from monographs on da Vinci and de Kooning to a collection of Calvin and Hobbes cartoons.

Elsewhere, gray metal cabinets hold artwork sorted by time and place. Open any drawer and brilliant pastels greet the eye. At the other end of the studio, on a raised section of the floor that was once the stage for school plays, a separate space serves as storage for canvases. Nearby, tacked to a wallboard, are three recent studies in acrylic of the surface of water. They shimmer.

A workbench is covered with painting materials: wide-mouth jars and coffee cans sprouting brushes; tubes of pigment in various stages of roll-up; turps; Q-tips; a box of purple latex gloves. Another table holds slide carousels, a light box, and art books Curry has been perusing. Among them is Alexander Eliot's *Three Hundred Years of American Painting,* which happens to be lying open to a reproduction of William Kienbusch's *The Weir and the Island.*

Like Curry, Kienbusch came to Maine, found his muse, and stayed. Kienbusch discovered "the world of many things I love—islands, trees, the sea, fences, gong buoys, churches, rocks, mountains." The first item on that list—islands—would be his grand theme, as it would be Curry's nearly a half century later.

A Life in Art

Curry's passion for making art began in his teenage years. While attending Hebron Academy in Maine in the mid-1970s, he took a class with sculptor Gary Ambrose. Ambrose's approach was simple: sit down with a piece of wood and see what materializes. This hands-on, fearless attitude appealed to Curry; for all the learning he has gained in the ensuing years, he continues to follow the dictates of freedom.

Entering the Rhode Island School of Design in 1977, Curry majored in sculpture. He began with clay modeling, then turned to wood carving and finally bronze. The hand-eye connection, the realization of form—these sculptural tenets would serve Curry well when he took up the brush.

Each year the School of Design offers a winter session during which students are encouraged to "jump" majors and take on an intensive study of another subject or discipline. In his freshman year, Curry signed up for a painting class with George Pappas, who instructed his students on how to see in color, represent gesture and motion, and tie together compositional elements. "This, to this, to this," Curry remembers Pappas saying as he demonstrated depth—foreground, middle ground, background.

Further studies set the foundation for Curry's growth as a painter and inspired him to explore figurative subjects. Study abroad also played a role in his artistic growth. In his junior year, Curry lived in Italy, where he absorbed centuries of art and architecture, humbled by the masterpieces of the past.

Following graduation in 1981, Curry attended Yale University to further develop skills of perception and draftsmanship. Yet, uncomfortable with the academic coursework, Curry eventually left Yale. He bought a French easel, a set of pastels, and moved to Hawaii.

In Honolulu, Curry met up with Bill Braden, a fellow Rhode Island School of Design graduate establishing himself as an eminent island painter. They traveled to different parts of Hawaii to tackle a variety of motifs. Curry fell in love with the *plein air* approach and with landscape. He also embraced pastel, enamored by the combination of drawing and color, and by the medium's intuitive quality.

After eight months in a Pacific paradise, Curry returned stateside, moving to Boston. He spent the next two years creating pastels of urban subjects—building exteriors, bridges, and the like. Barely scraping by, he applied to graduate school at the University of Massachusetts at Amherst, where he could teach in exchange for tuition.

As had happened in Hawaii, the landscape called. Finishing classes for the day, Curry would drive to the Connecticut River to paint. It was there he began to understand color. One day, he discovered he had brought only reds and yellows, so he drew the landscape using just the two colors. This experience helped move him into more expressive realms.

Curry also took trips to New York City to study the masters in the Metropolitan Museum of Art. Among the artists he returned to time and again was Edgar Degas. The great French painter's pastels taught him about layering and deepened his appreciation of the range of effects this medium was capable of producing.

After finishing graduate school in 1987, Curry married and moved with Kimberly to a house in Somerville, Massachusetts. He worked part-time in computer graphics and continued to paint. In 1995, Kimberly was offered the editorship of a new magazine, *Hope,* published by *Wooden Boat* magazine in Brooklin, Maine. The couple decided to make the move. Curry remembers being somewhat distressed about leaving his relatively comfortable life on the outskirts of Boston. Any reservations quickly disappeared. Looking back, he considers the move to Maine something of a homecoming.

Through his remarkable island paintings and a stunning collection of pastels, Curry has taken his place in an esteemed line of Maine coast artists and in the broader lineage of distinguished American landscape painters. Discipline and dedication have served him well, as has a commitment to exploring new avenues of art.

"To cleave that sea in the gentle autumnal season, murmuring the name of each islet, is to my mind the joy most apt to transport the heart to paradise."

—Nikos

Morning After the Storm, oil on panel, 36" x 43", collection of John Randall.

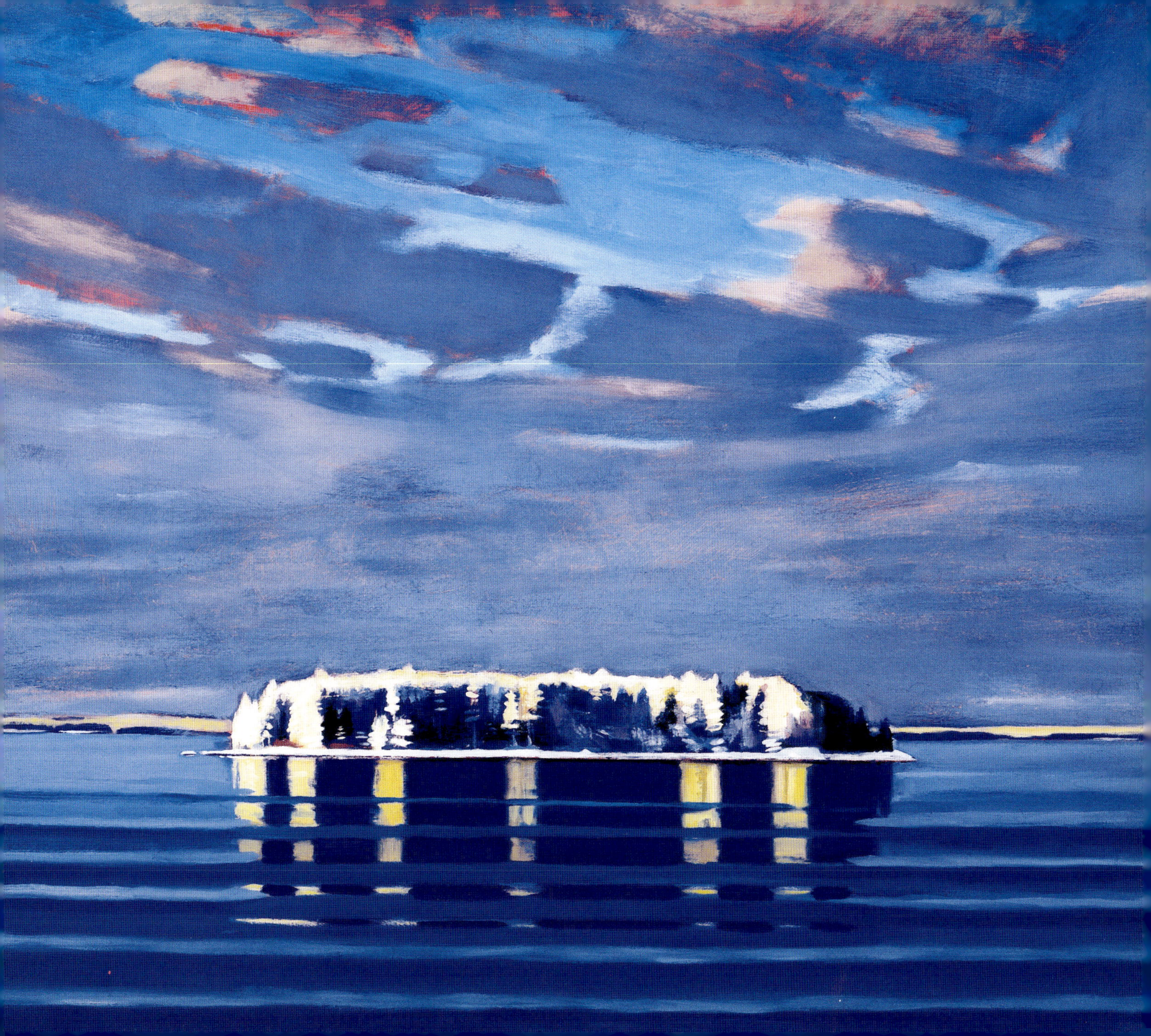

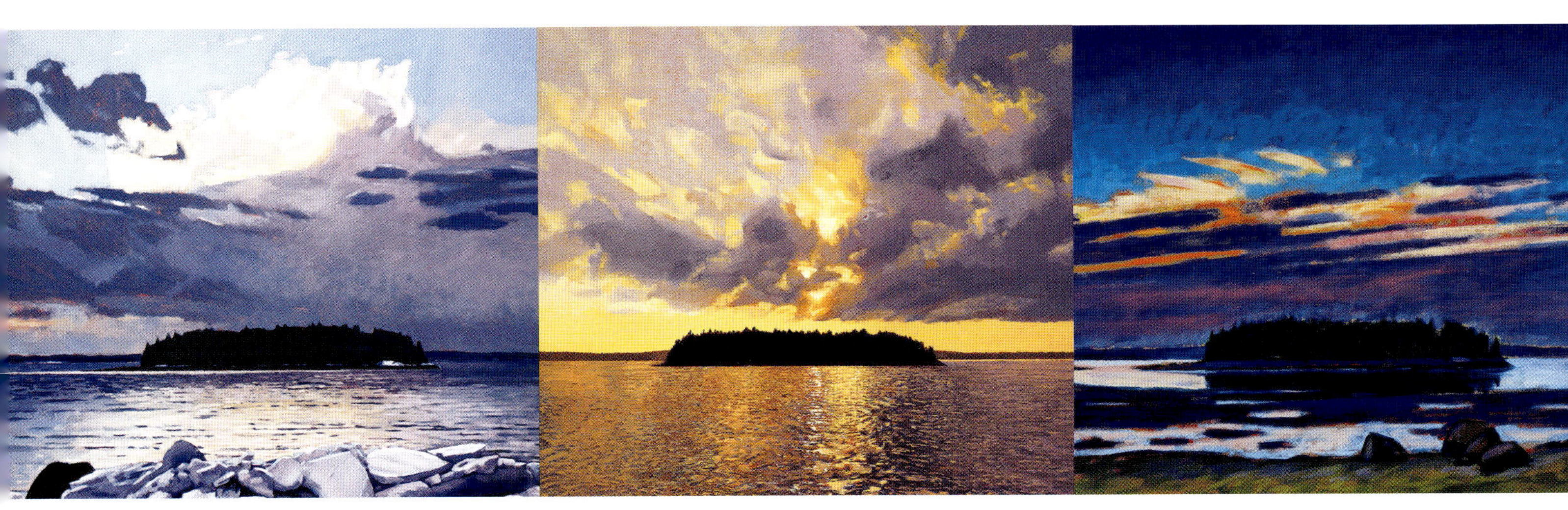

Crossing the Water

Tom Curry

I've always had a deep fear of the ocean. It began when I was a child splashing in the sea with my mother. A powerful wave knocked us both over, and in trying to regain her balance, my mother accidentally pinned me under the water. I struggled to find footing.

The panic of that struggle seeped into my dreams. I would lie awake in bed, terrified of a recurring dream in which everything became vast and then miniscule. I felt the dark, cold weight of the sea smothering me.

The dream stopped eventually and my fear of water faded until my wife and I moved to the coast of Maine. We rented a house overlooking Eggemoggin Reach and a small, uninhabited island. Rowing out to the island one day, my heart started to race and I was struck by panic.

From then on, I rarely ventured across the water. I watched the island from shore, day and night. It defined my horizon: pulsing with the first orange light of dawn, darkened by storm clouds, glittering with ice after a winter storm.

At first, the island was merely my reference point, revealing the lay of the light, the direction of the wind, the rise and ebb of the tide. I consulted it to determine where to paint that day, depending on which places would provide a lee against the wind or whether the tide was coming or going.

Within a few years, however, the winter darkness gained a strong hold on me and I decided to explore my fear of water head on. The island became my subject. It encapsulated my dark projections sitting in a far-off world. I started painting the island as a way to delve into my own darkness and seek a way back to the surface.

As I began to paint, a narrative emerged: island as escape and entrapment, island as longing and memory, island as self, island as sanctuary in a sea of turmoil. These paintings aren't so much landscapes as they are portraits. They are also meditations on the dance between immutability and flux.

The island has become a constant presence in my life. It draws my gaze across the water every time I walk down to the shore. It is layered in memories of light, wind, and water, which inform this series of paintings. In mid-winter, the island and shoreline are rimmed with huge sheaths of ice half-submerged in water tinted green with blooming plankton. On a late spring afternoon, the island hunkers beneath gathering storm clouds, awaiting the deluge. On a summer morning, a scrim of fog nearly obscures the island as ghostly, skeletal boat cradles drift in the foreground.

The vastness of the sea still steals my breath. But perhaps separateness, like an island, is only an illusion. As Kathleen Dean Moore writes, an island is ". . . only a high point in the continuous skin of the planet, the small part we can see of the hidden substance that connects everything on earth. It's a sign . . . of the wholeness of being, the intricate interdependencies that link people and place."

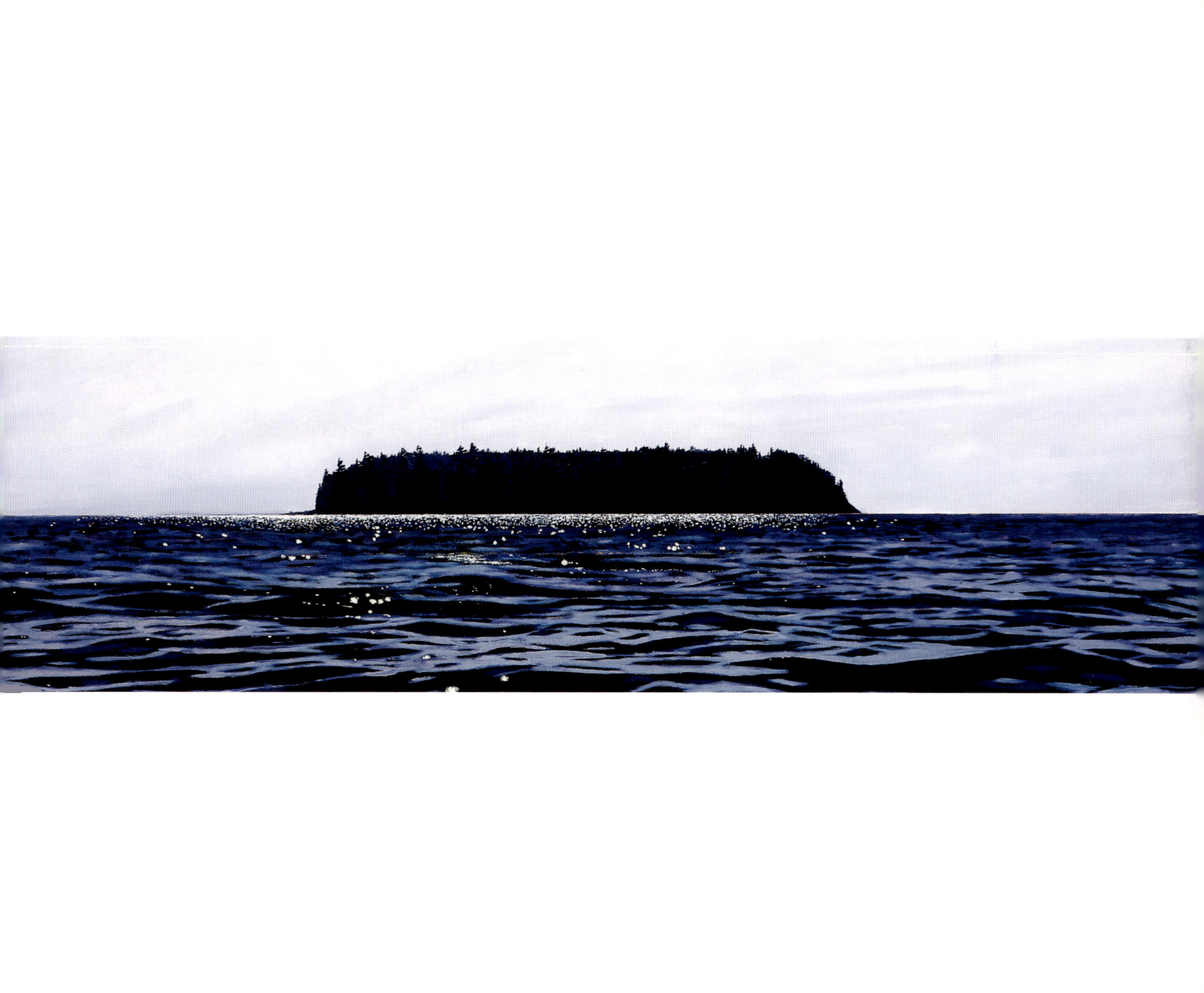

"The cold remote islands

And the blue estuaries

Where what breathes, breathes

The restless wind of the inlets,

And what drinks, drinks

The incoming tide . . ."

—Louise Bogan, from "Night"

January, oil on panel, 36" x 43", collection of the artist.

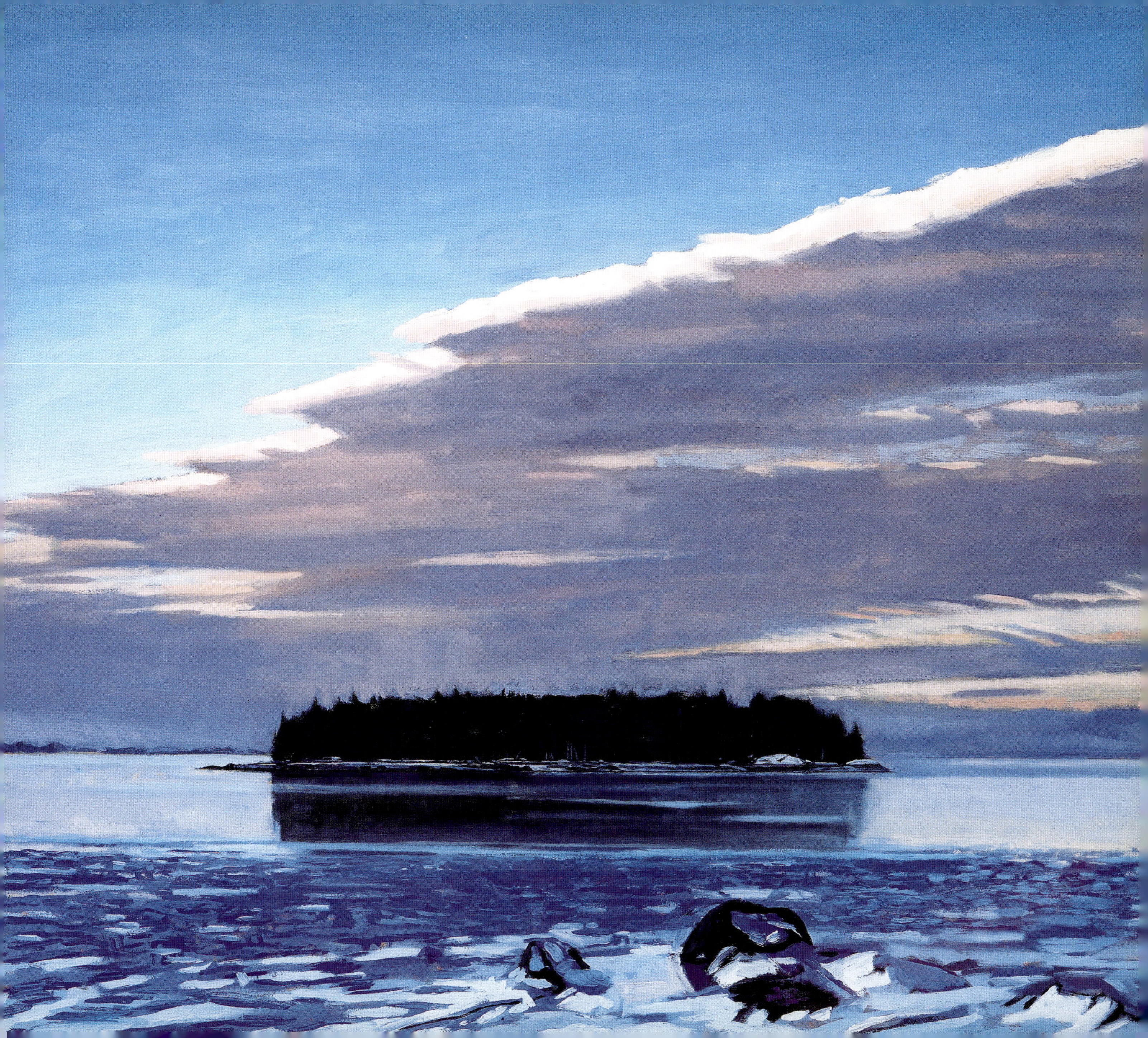

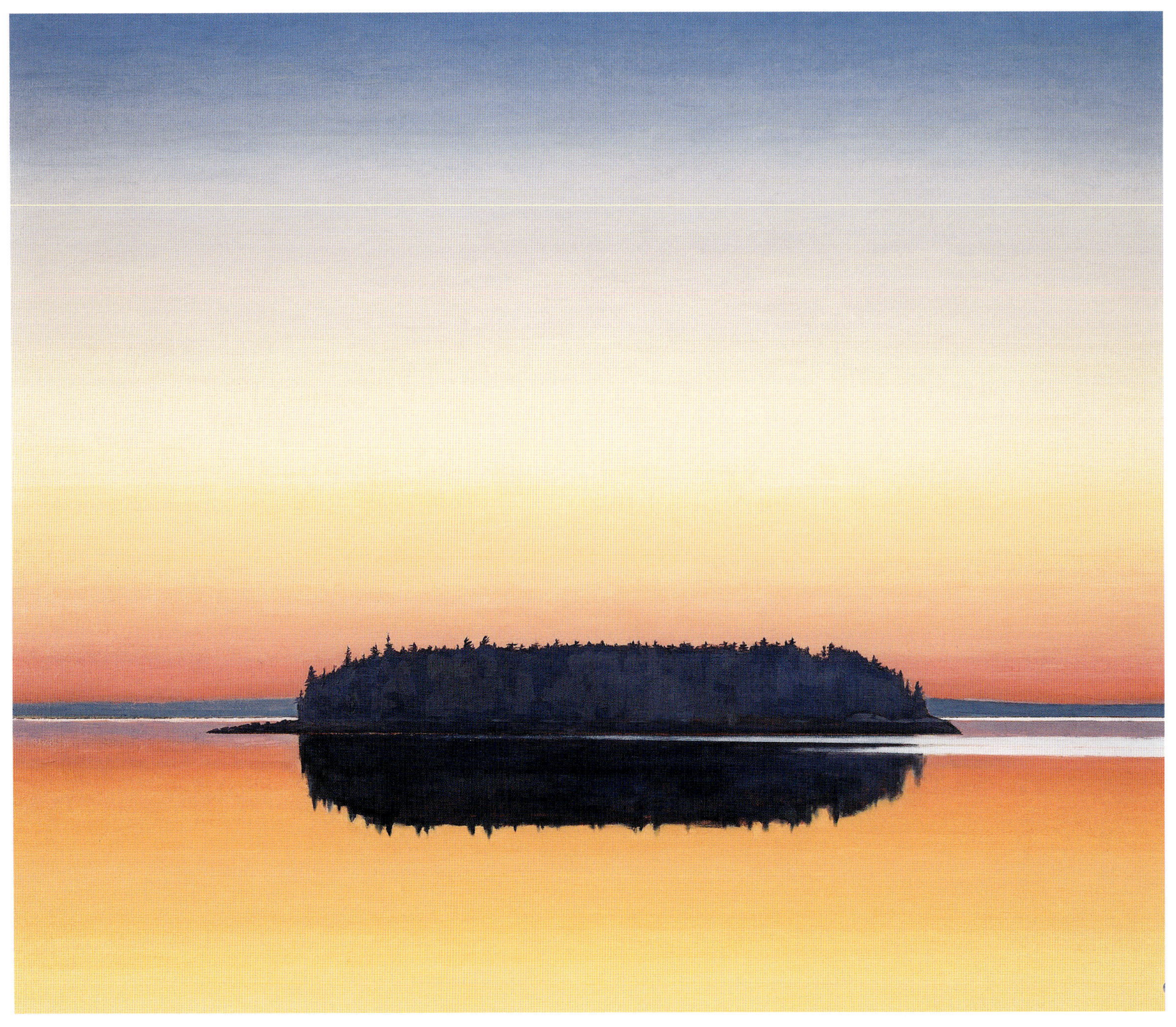

Crimson Sky, oil on panel, 36" x 43", collection of Randy and Pam Phelps.

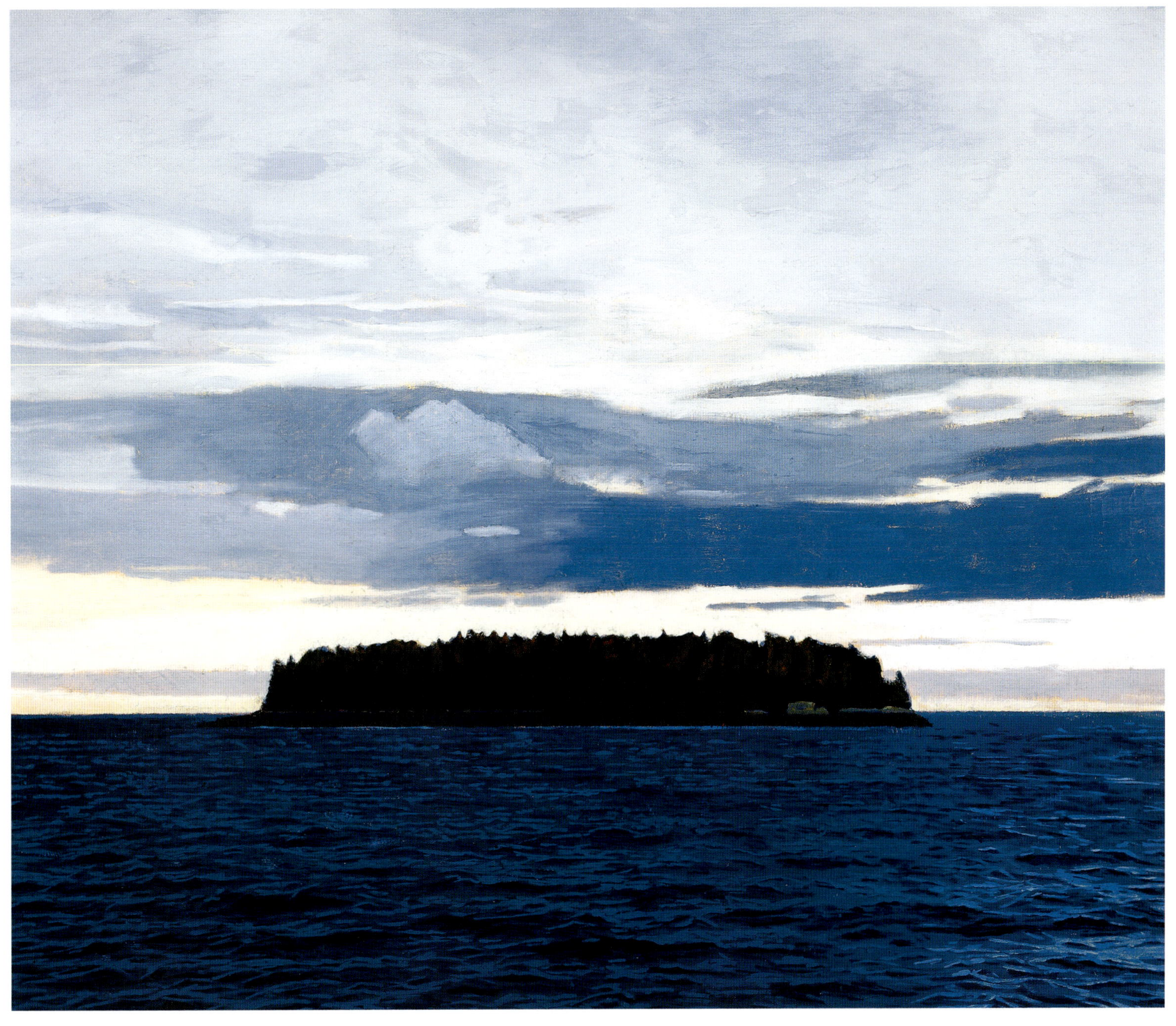

September Evening, oil on panel, 36" x 43", collection of Nancy and Bucky Kales.

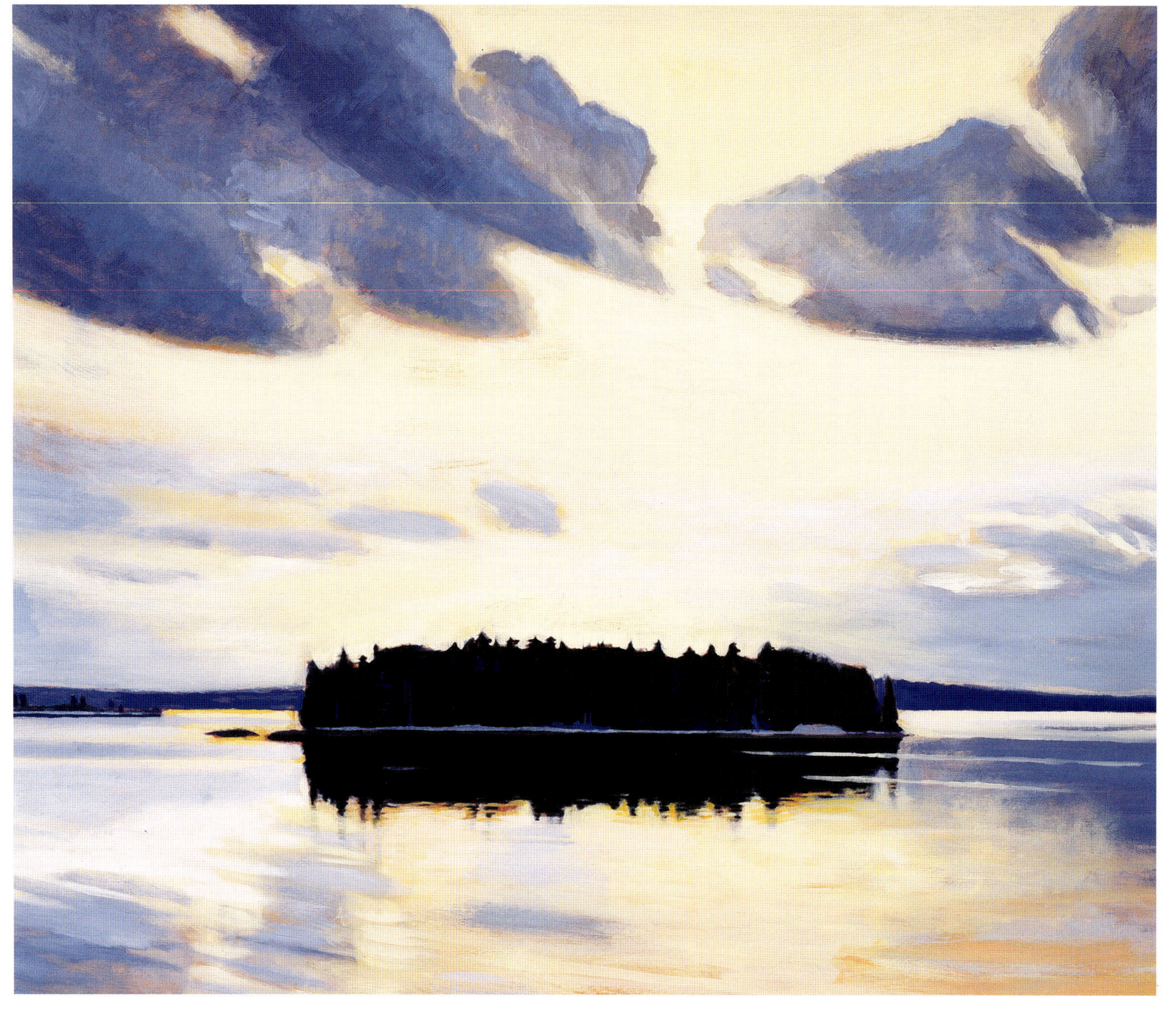

Chatto Island Sunset, oil on panel, 36" x 43", collection of Hanna Henderson.

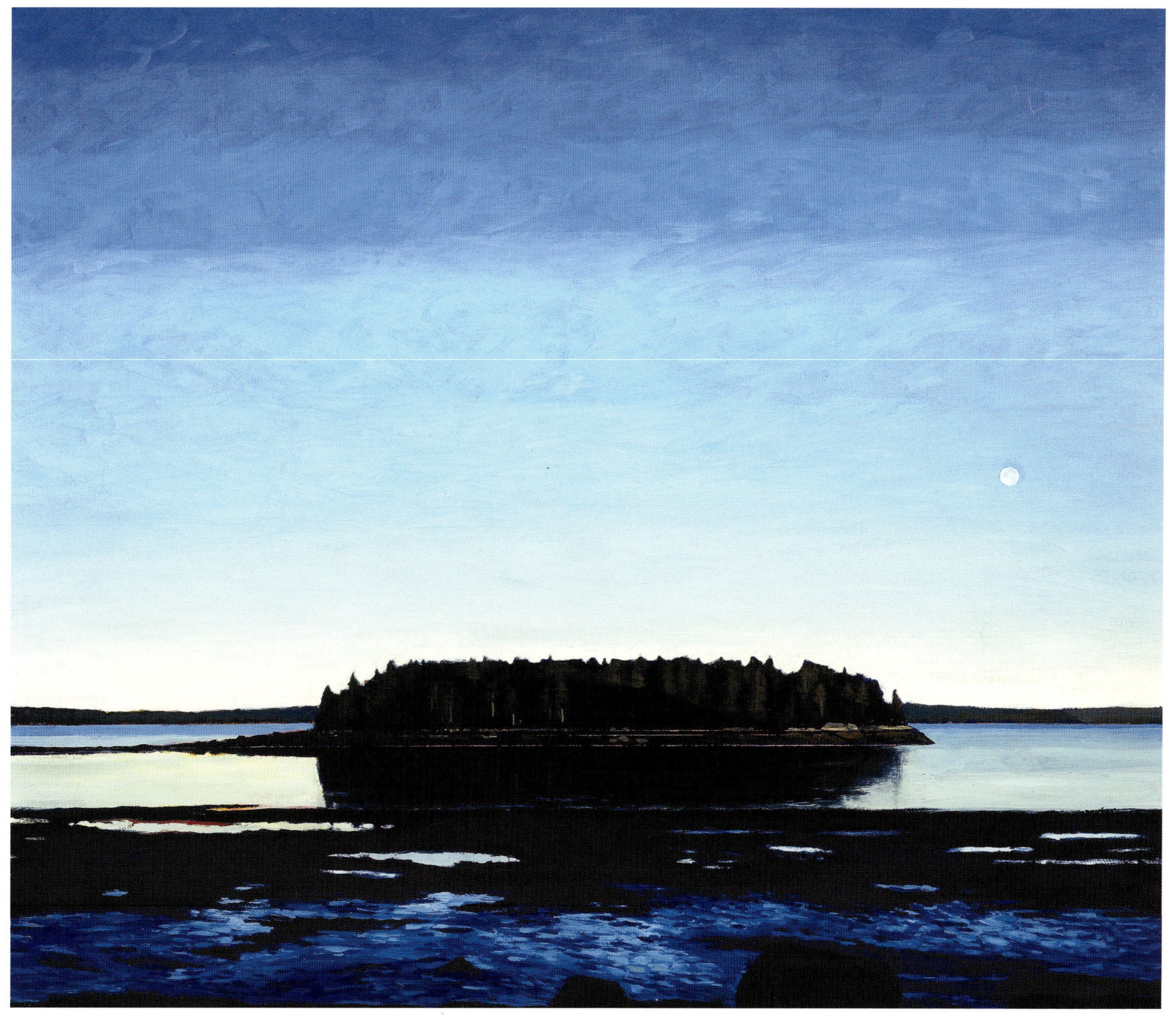

Morning Moon, oil on panel, 36" x 43", collection of Nancy and Bucky Kales. overleaf: *Blue Mist,* oil on panel, 36" x 43", Cigliano/Hartman collection.

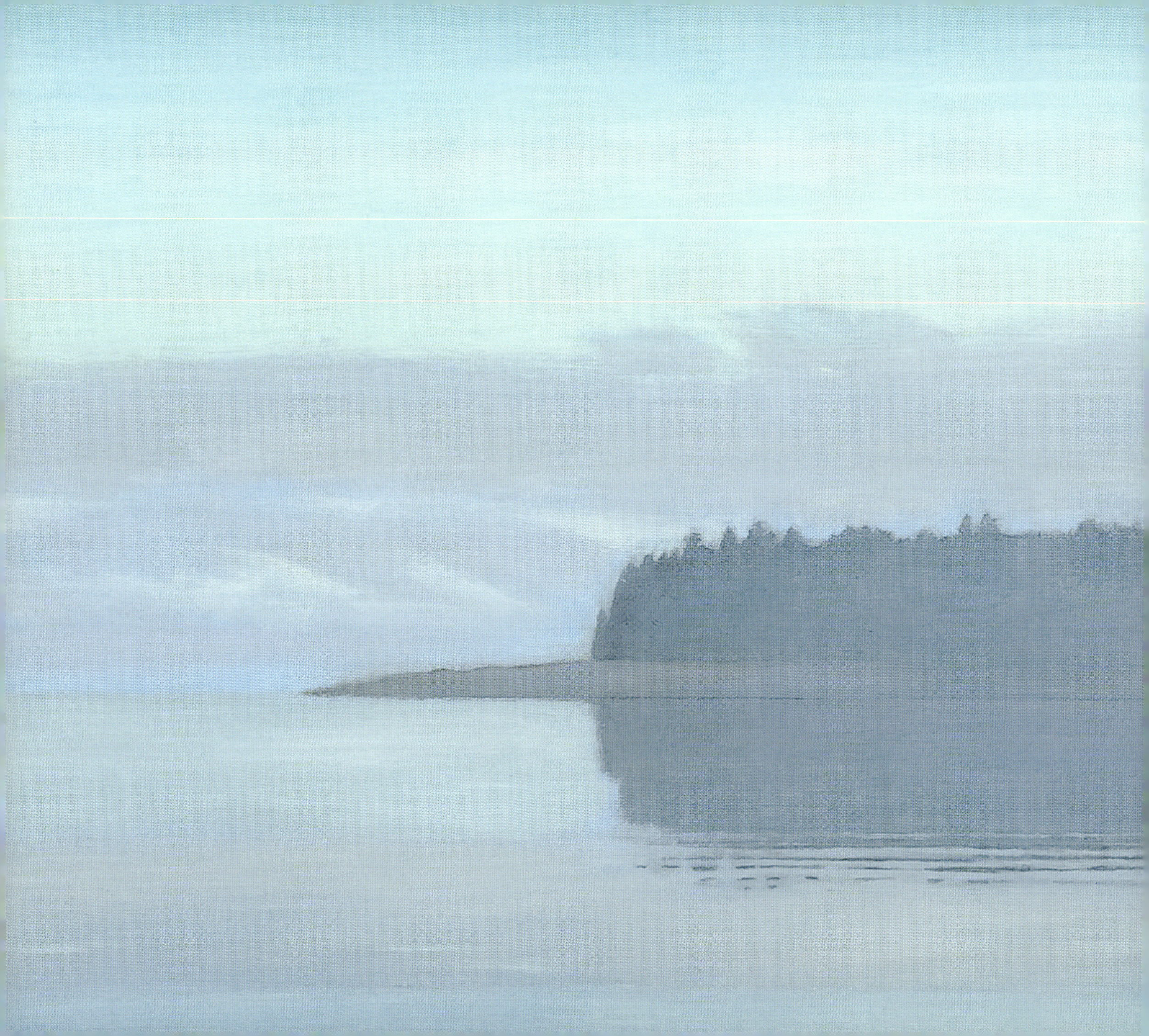

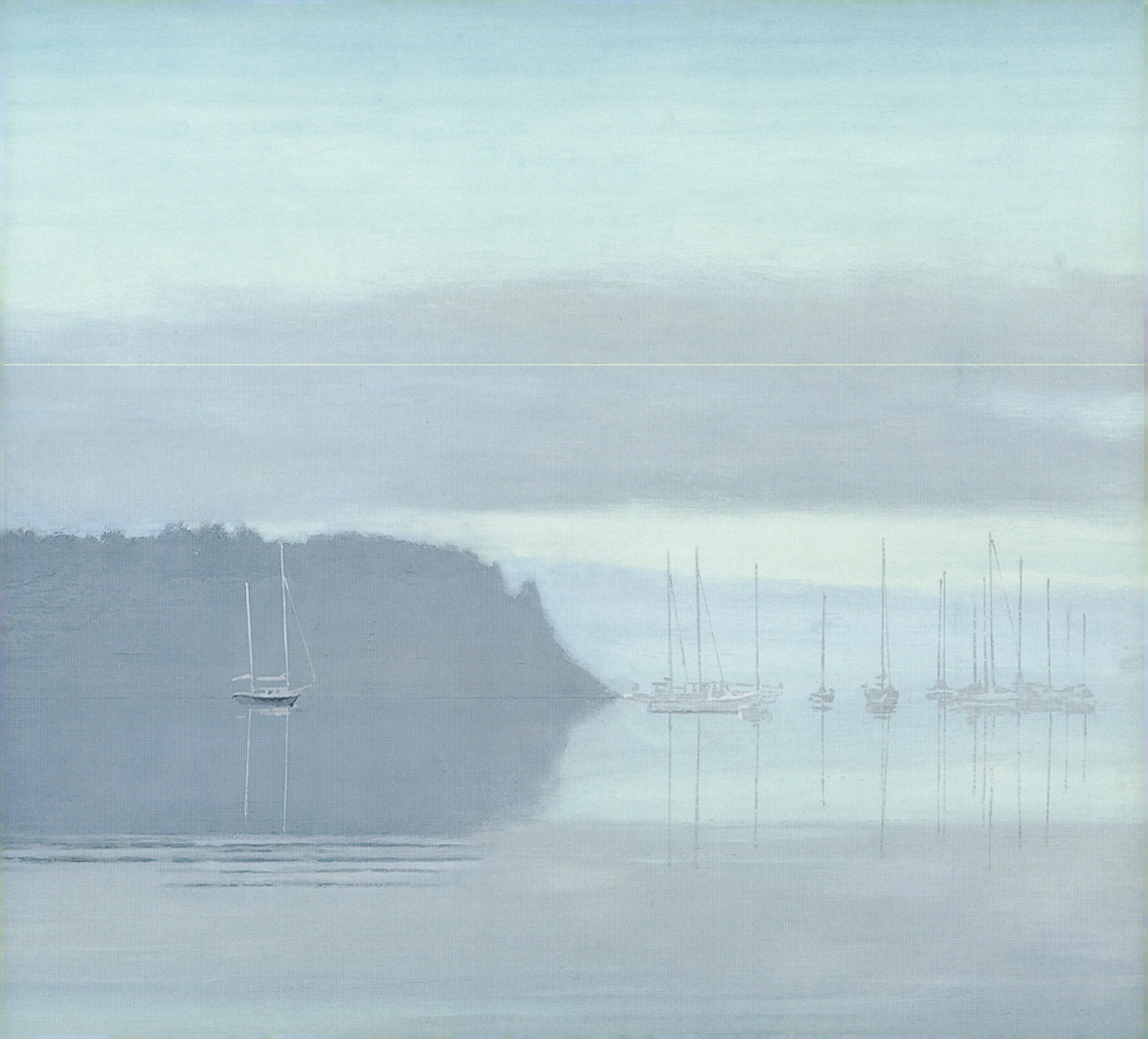

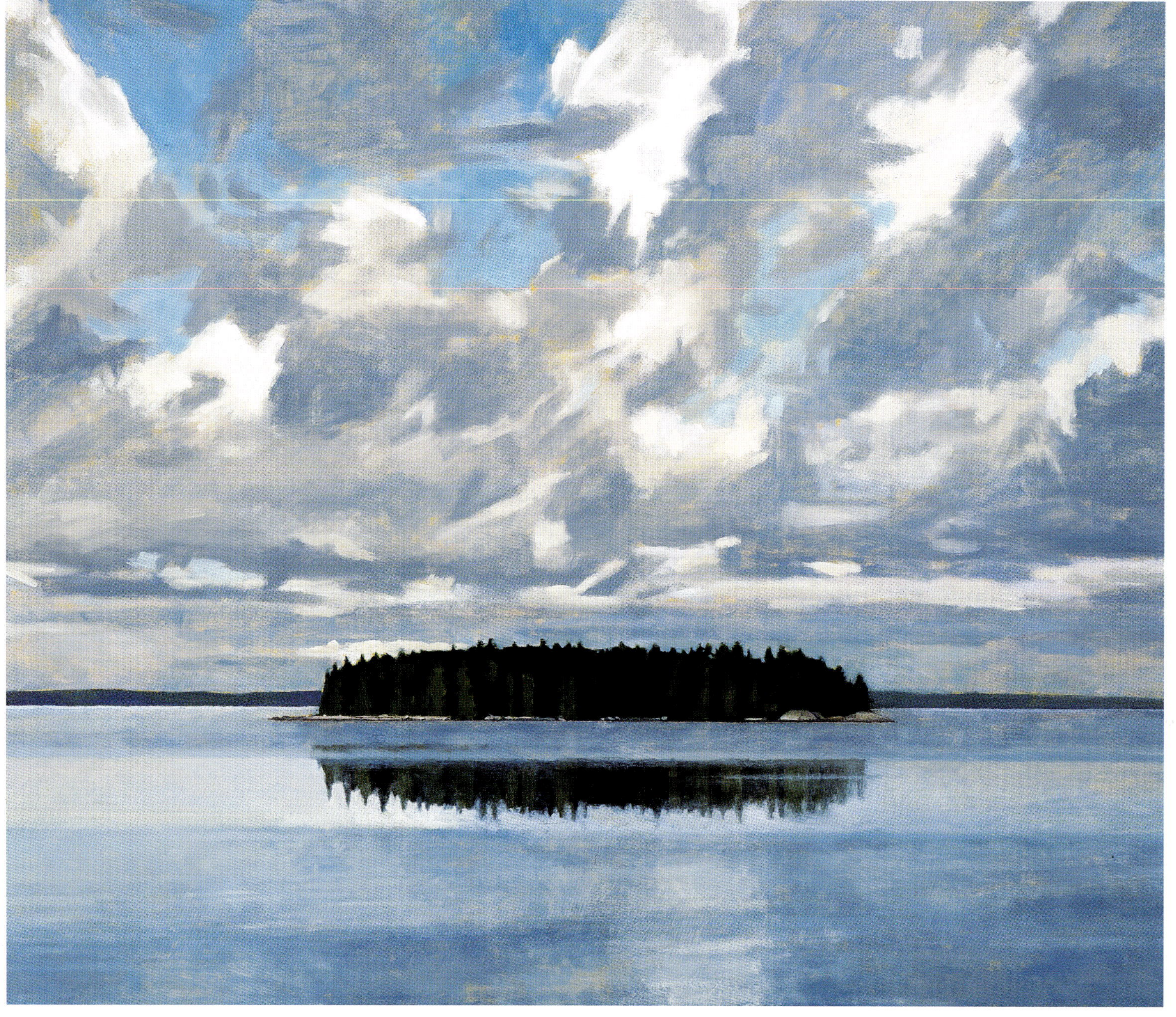

Big Sky, oil on panel, 36" x 43", collection of Karla Austen.

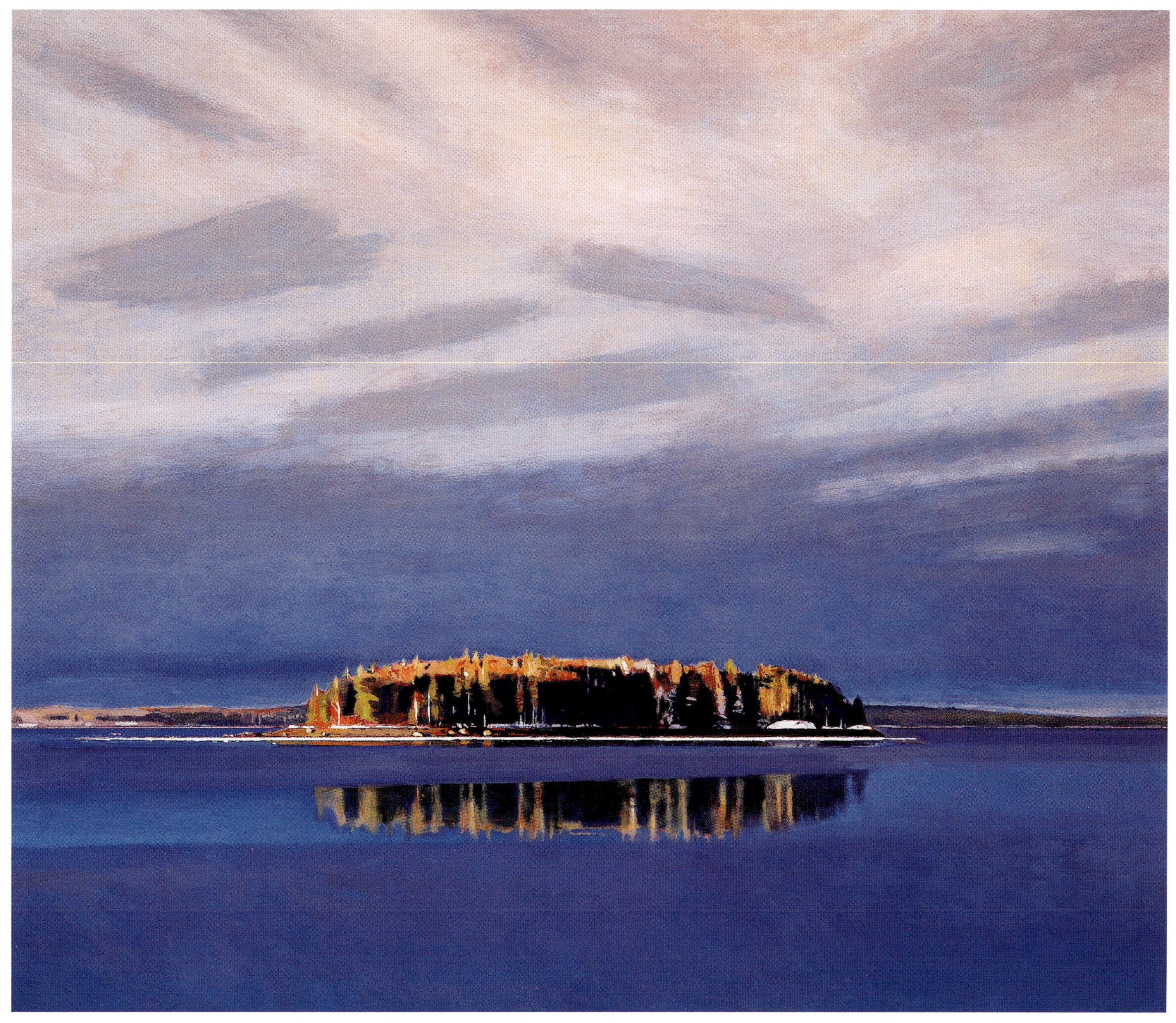

October Sky, oil on panel, 36" x 43", collection of Ann and Bill Harrison.

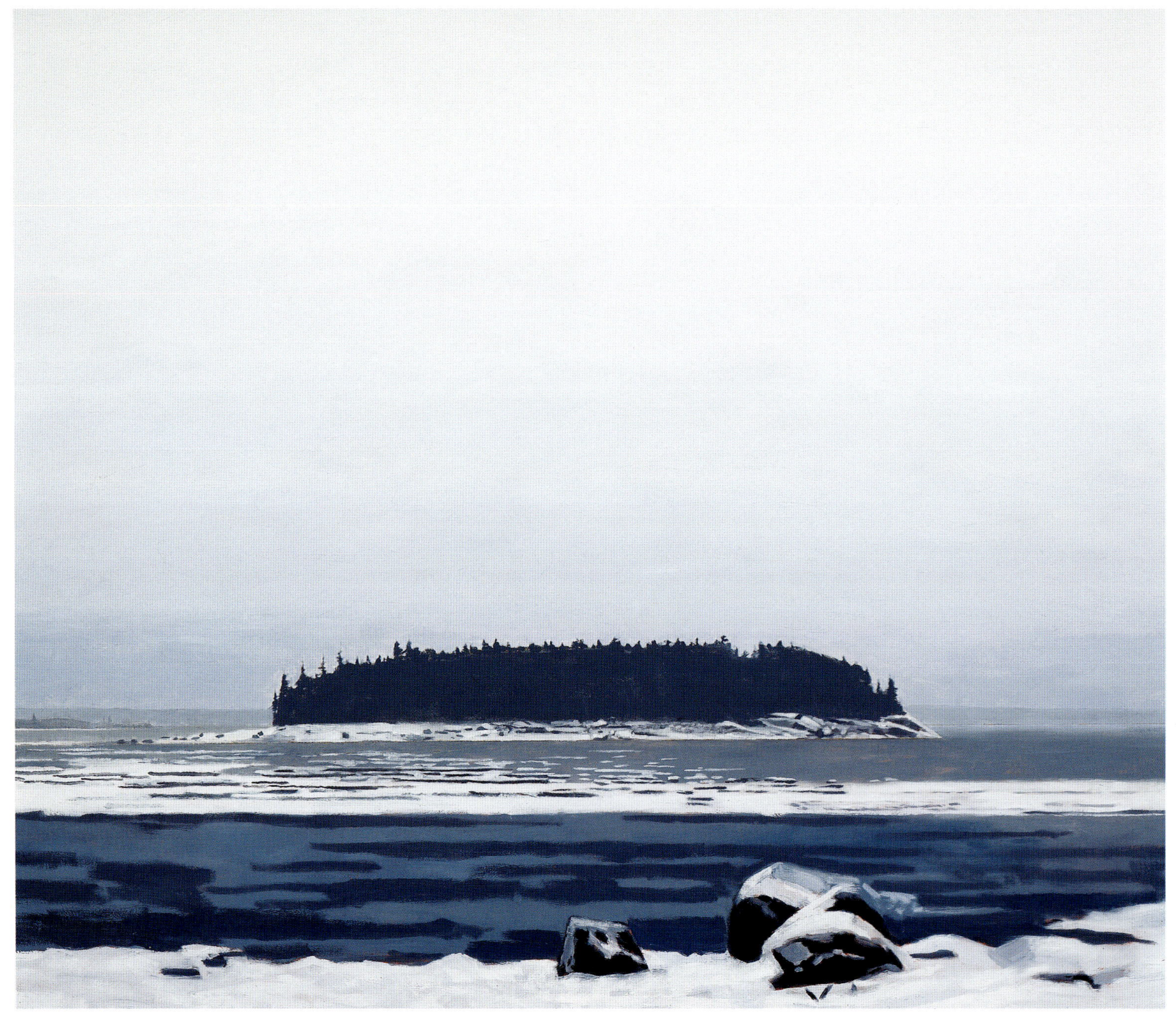

Blizzard, oil on panel, 36" x 43", collection of the artist.

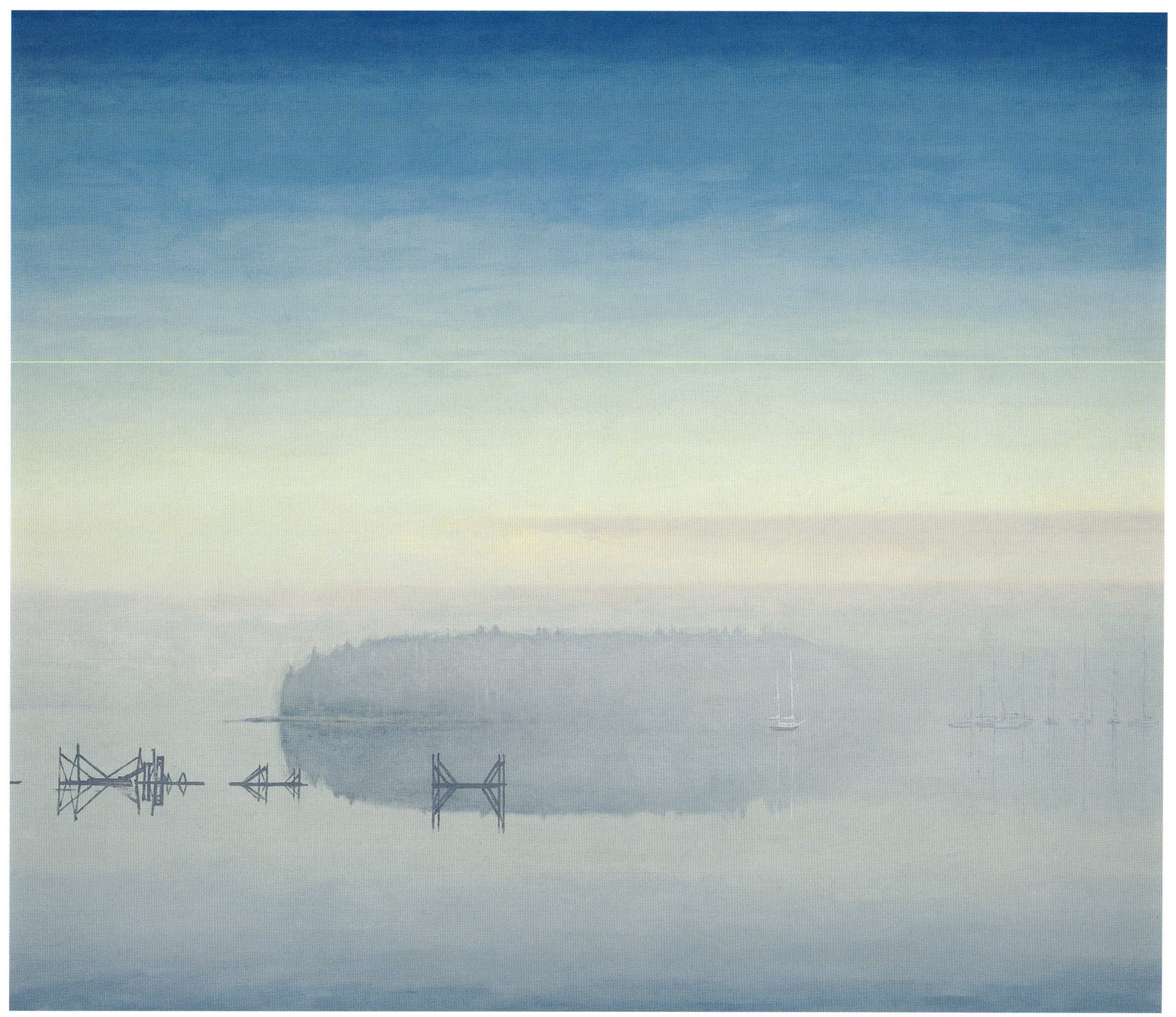

Morning Mist on Cradles, oil on panel, 48" x 57", collection of Nancy and Bucky Kales.

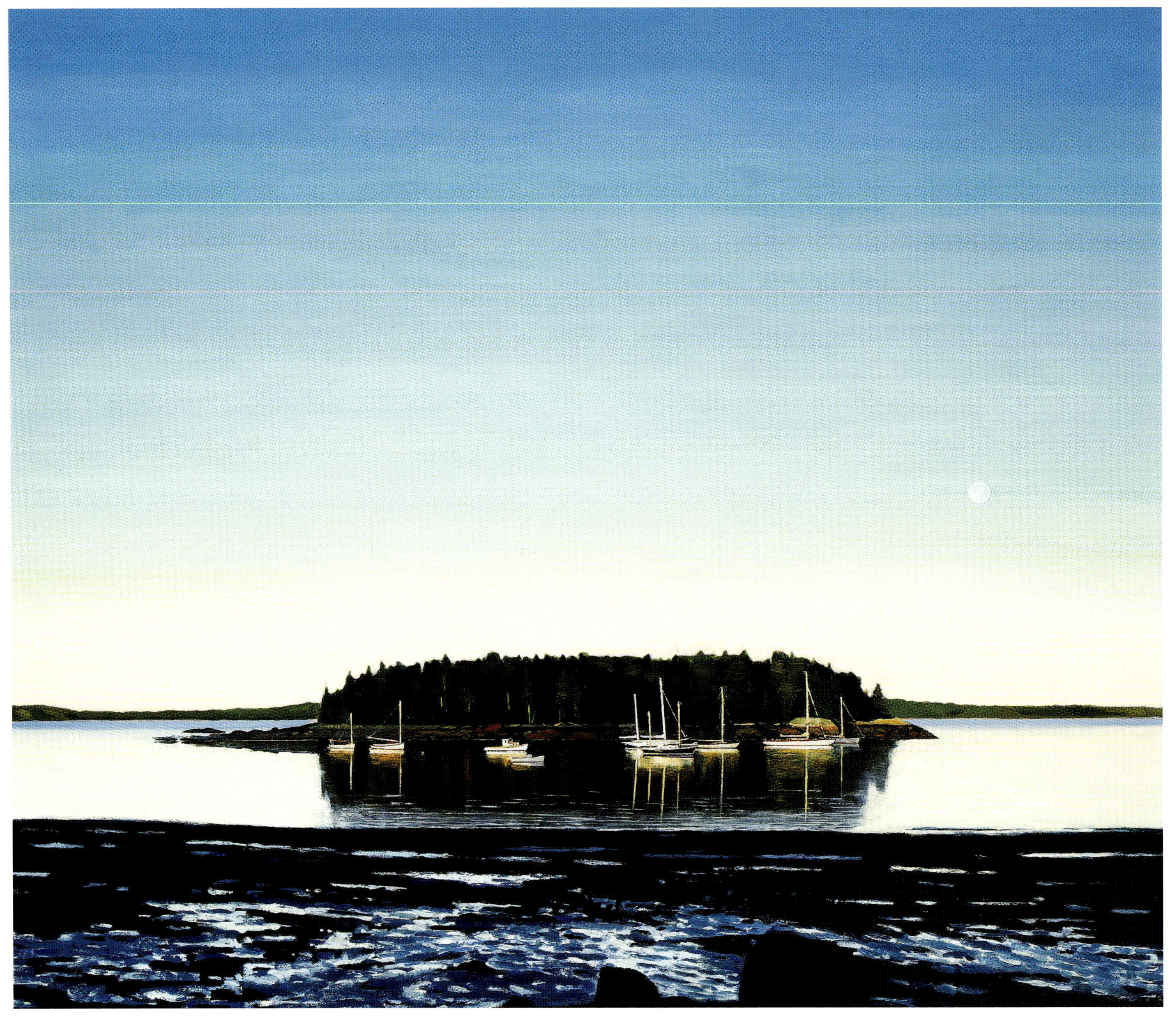

Center Harbor, oil on panel, 36" x 43", collection of Virginia Welles.

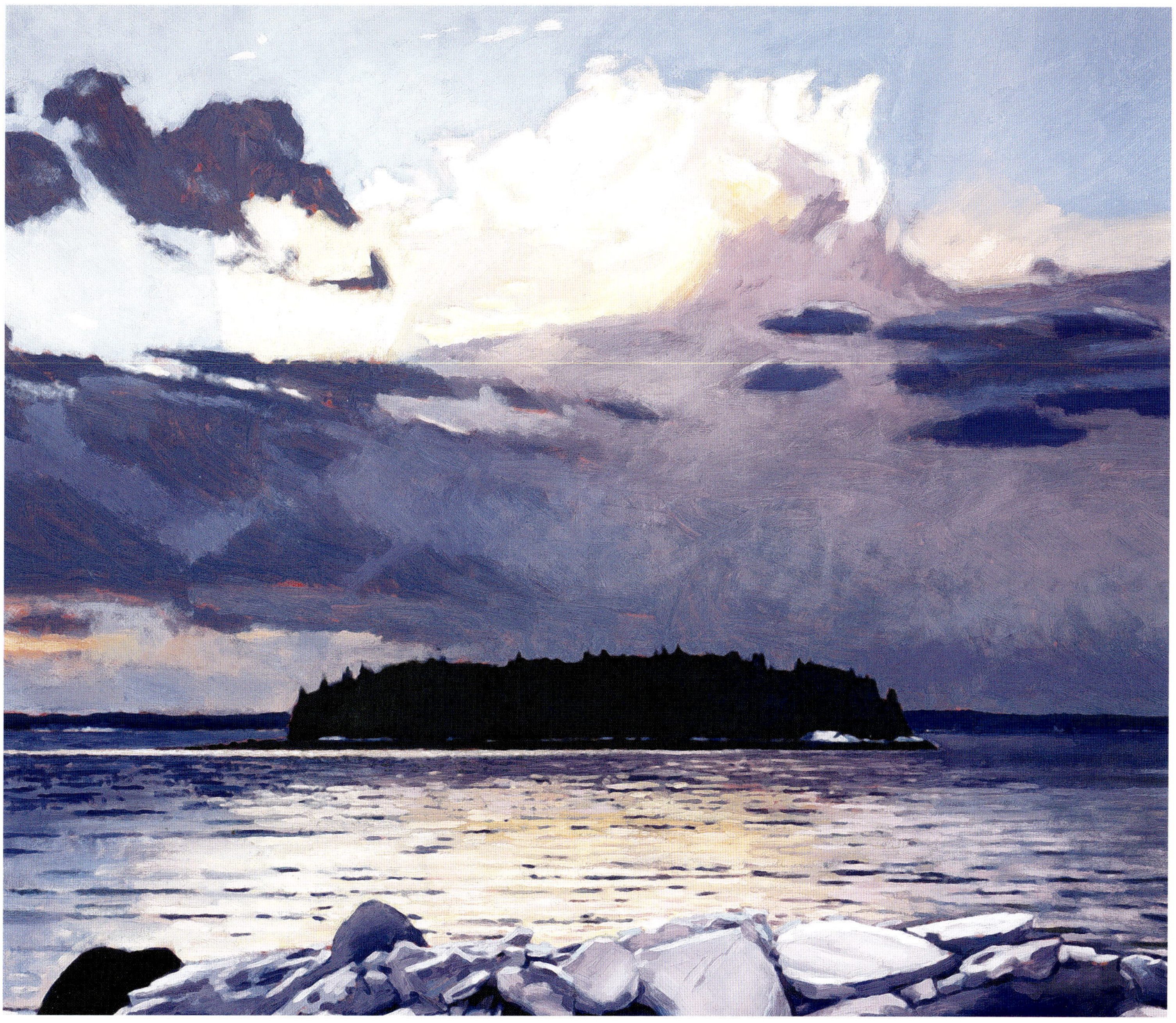

Frozen Sea, oil on panel, 36" x 43", collection of the artist.

overleaf: *Fair Winds* oil on panel, 36" x 43", collection of the artist.

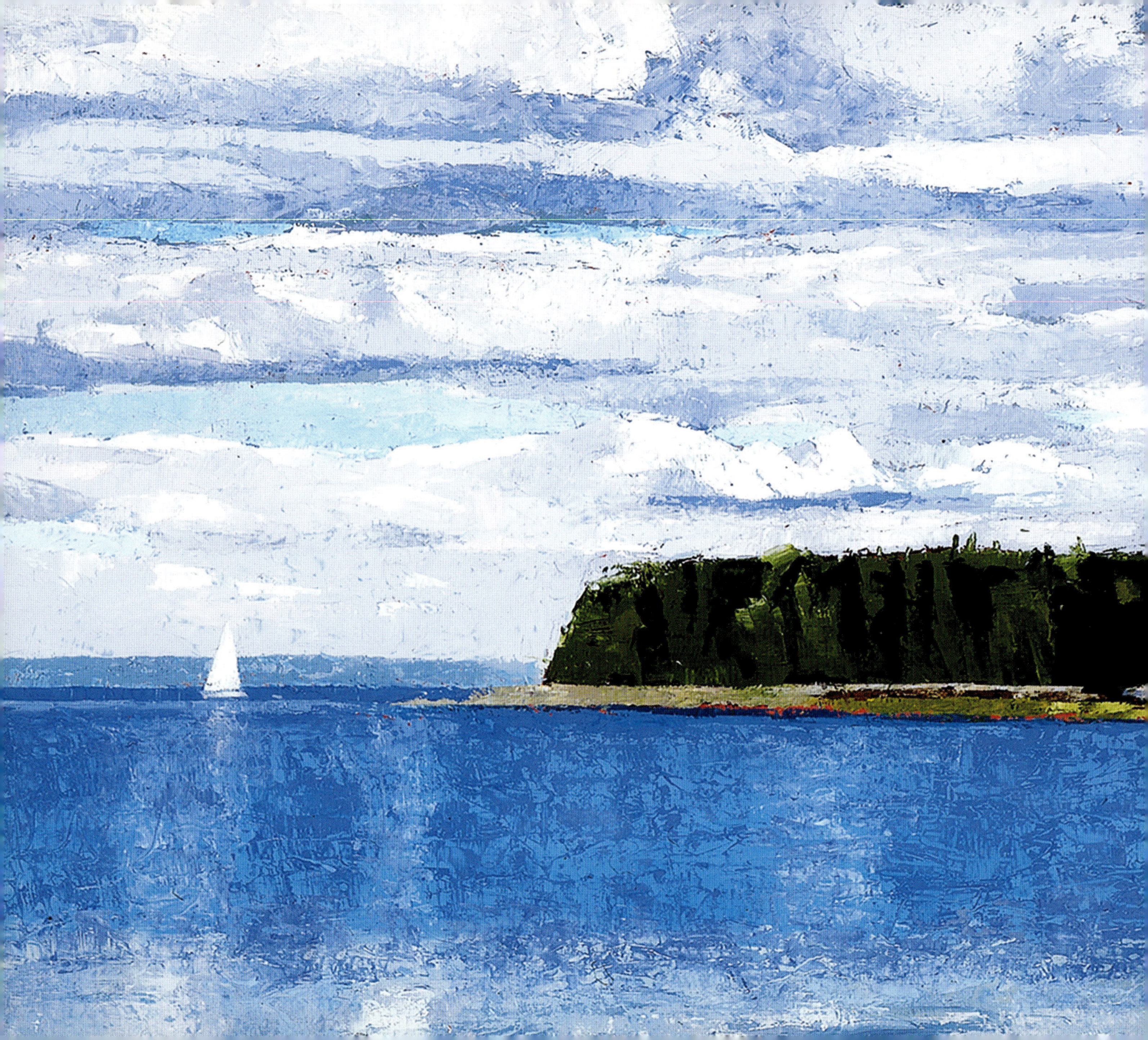

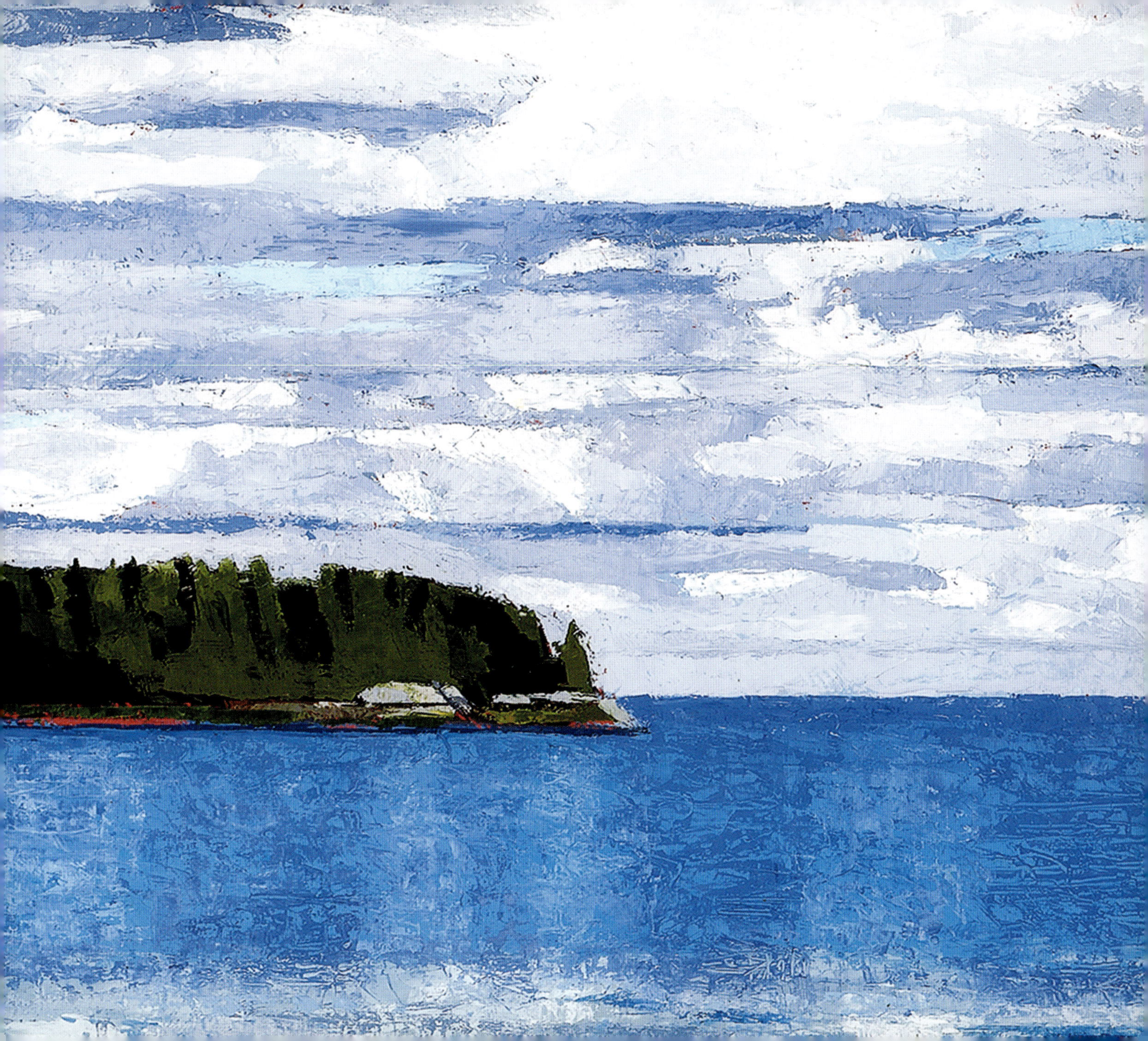

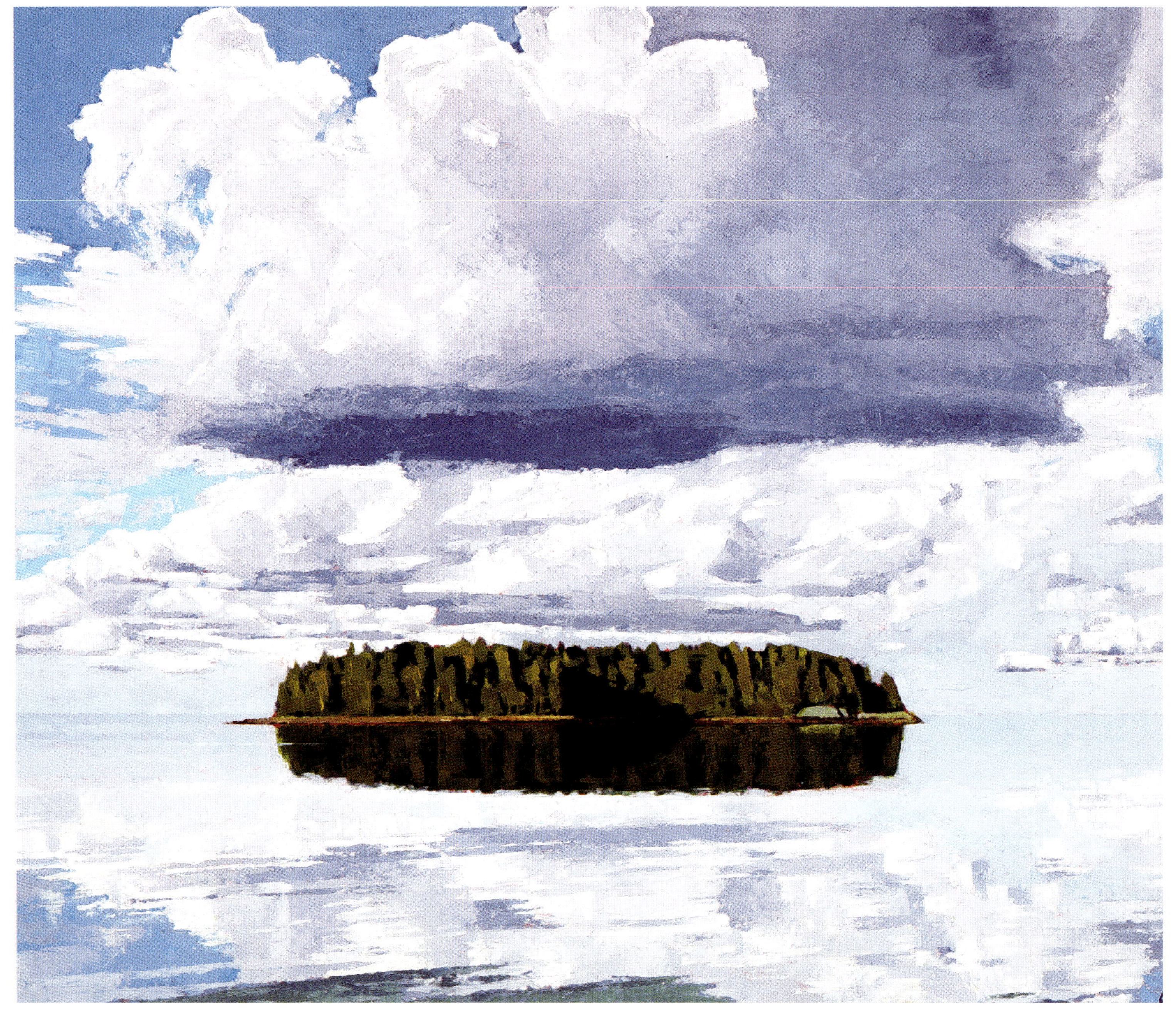

Stillness, oil on panel, 36" x 43", collection of the artist.

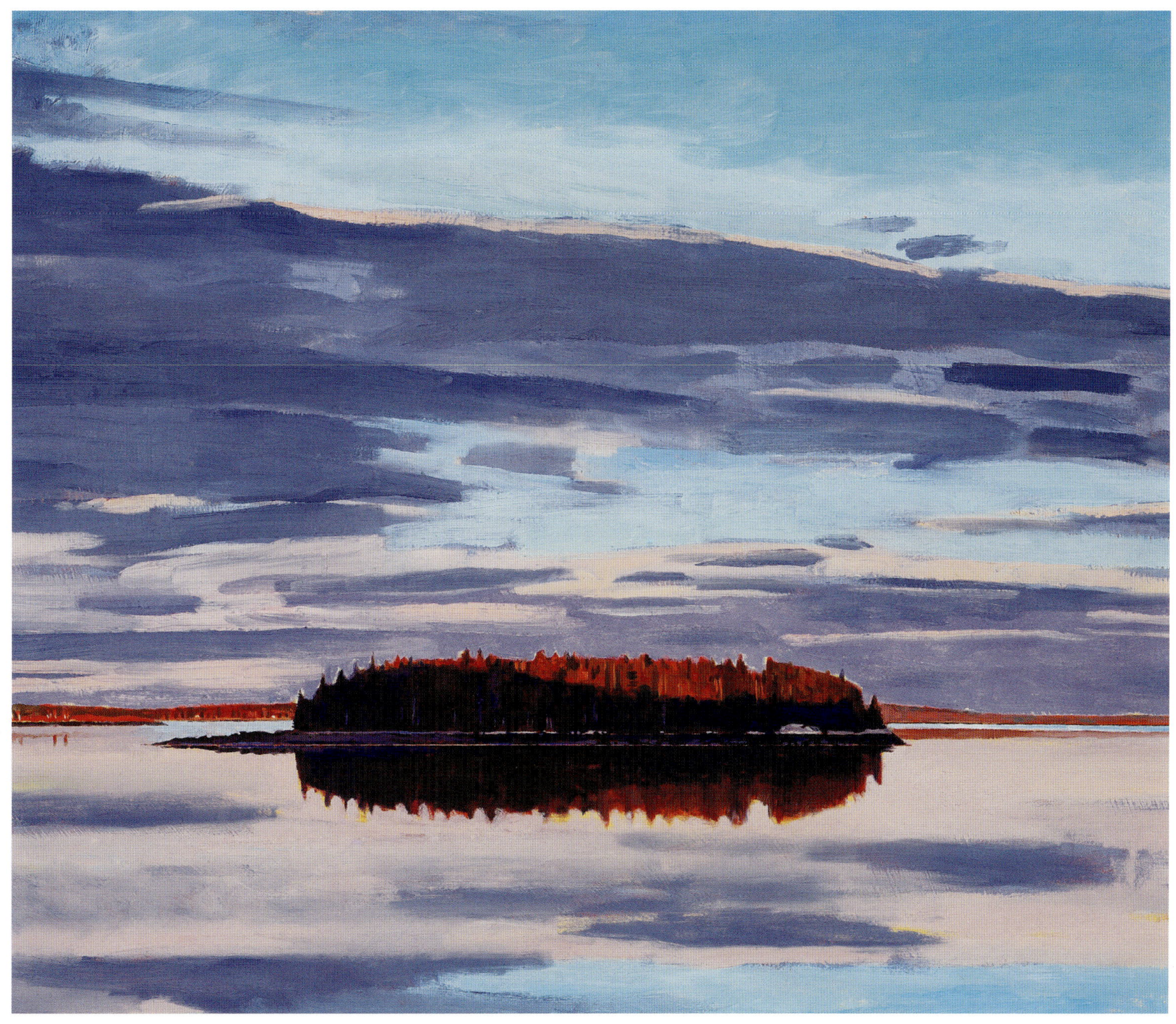

First Light, oil on canvas, 30" x 36", collection of the artist.

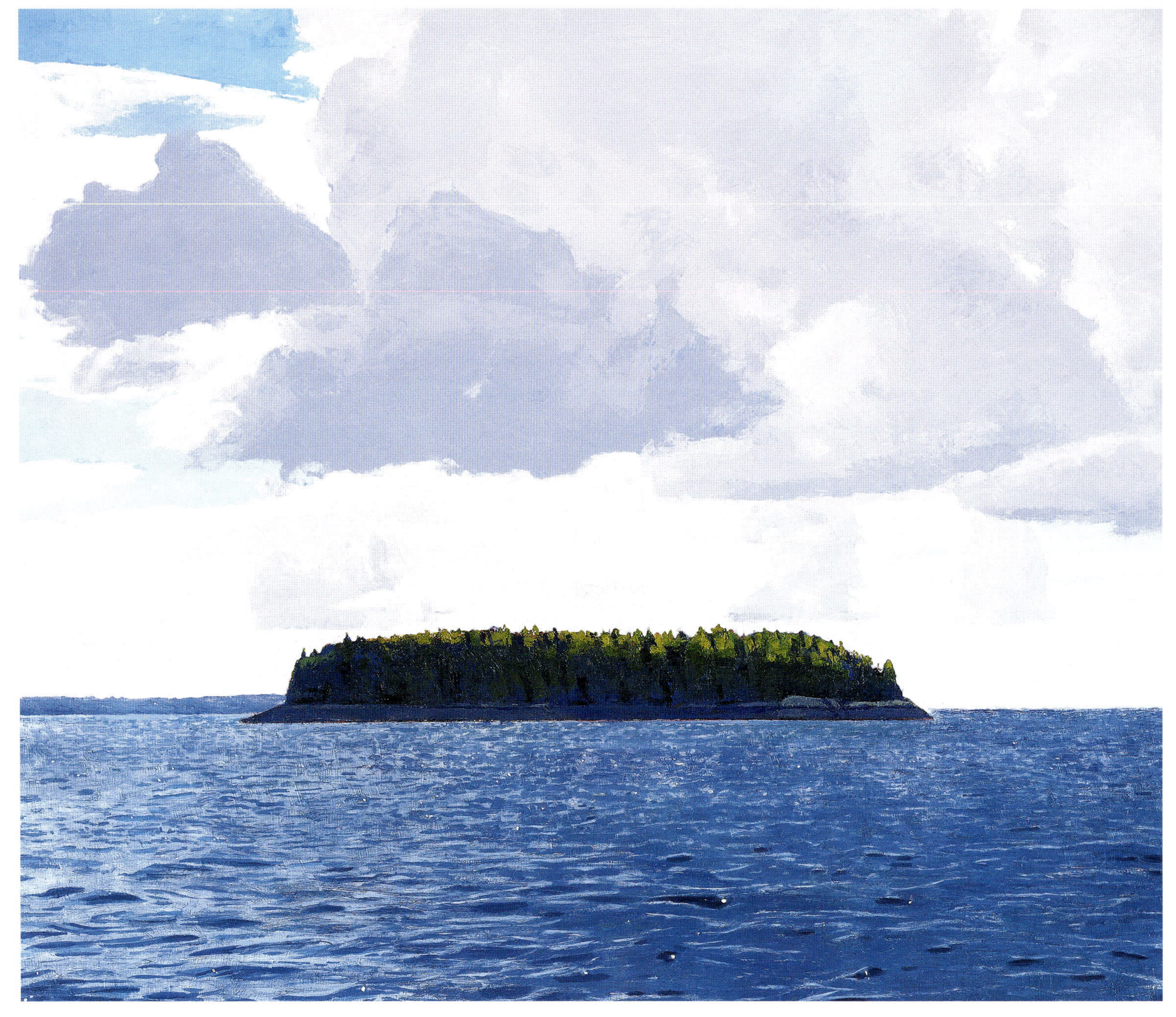

Gathering Clouds, oil on panel, 36" x 43", collection of Emma Littlejohn.

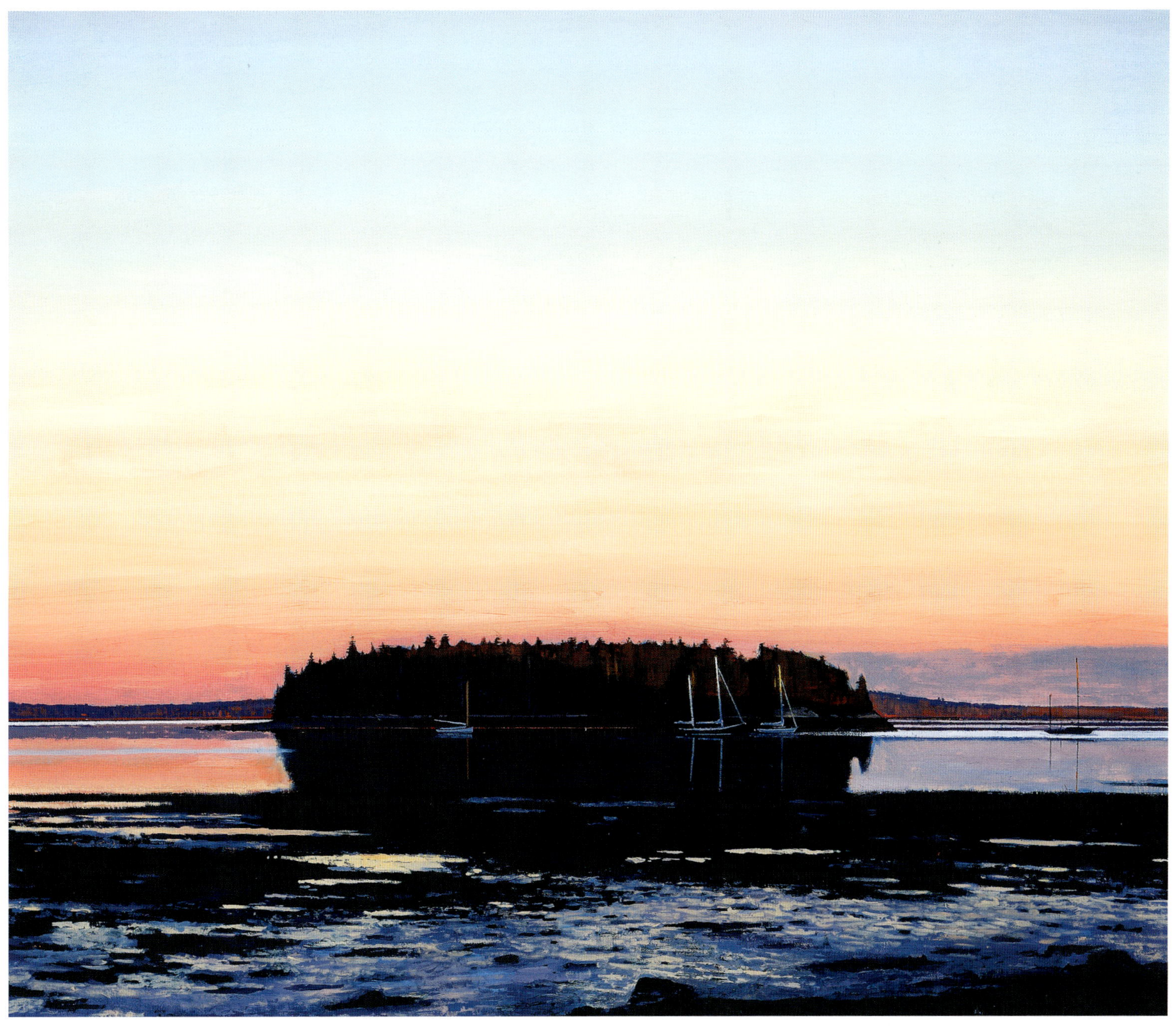

Dawn, oil on panel, 36" x 43", collection of Susan and George Schreiber.

Fog, oil on panel, 36" x 43", private collection.

Foggy Morning, oil on panel, 36" x 43", collection of the artist.

overleaf: *Chatto Island,* oil on panel, 36" x 43". collection of Nick and Cassandra Ludington.

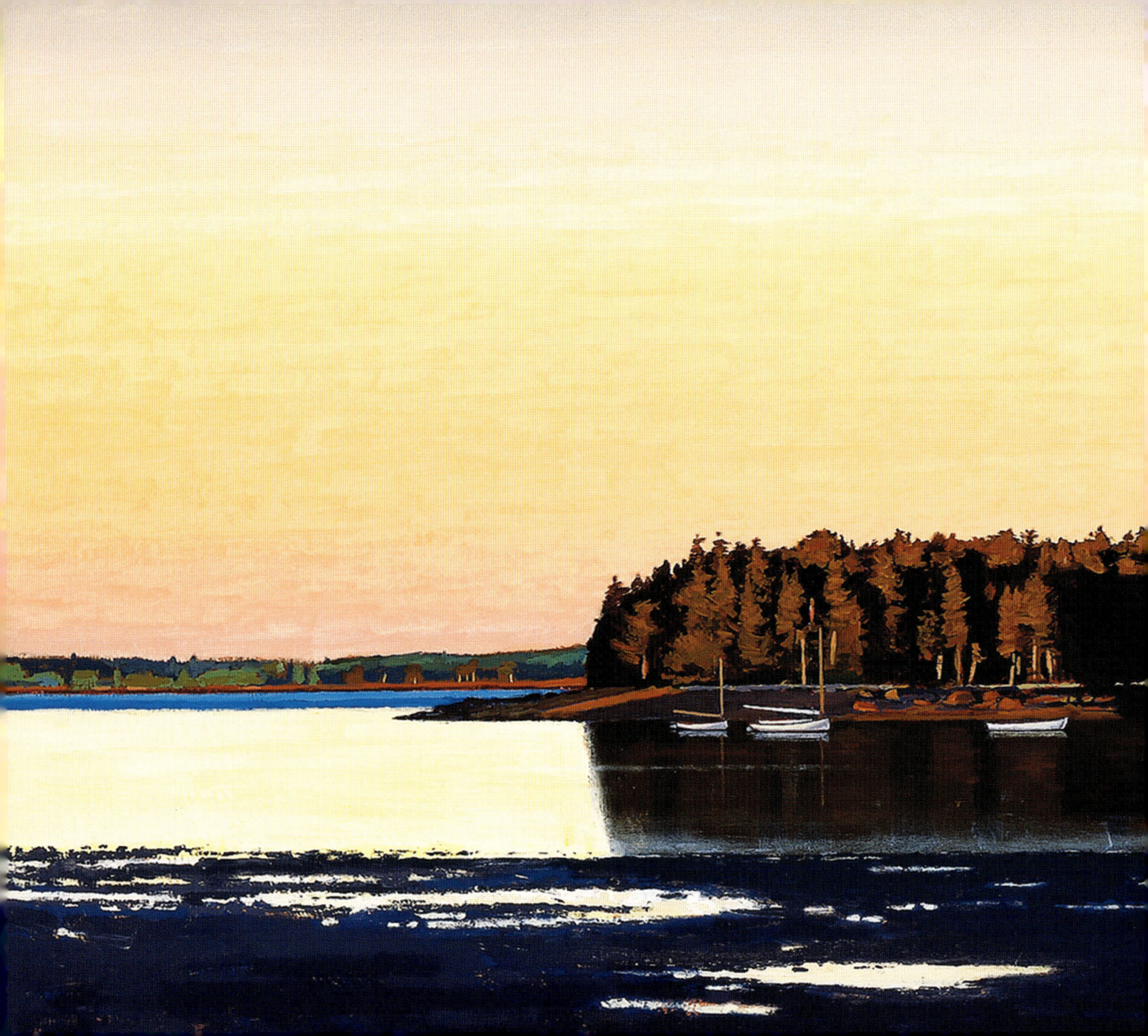

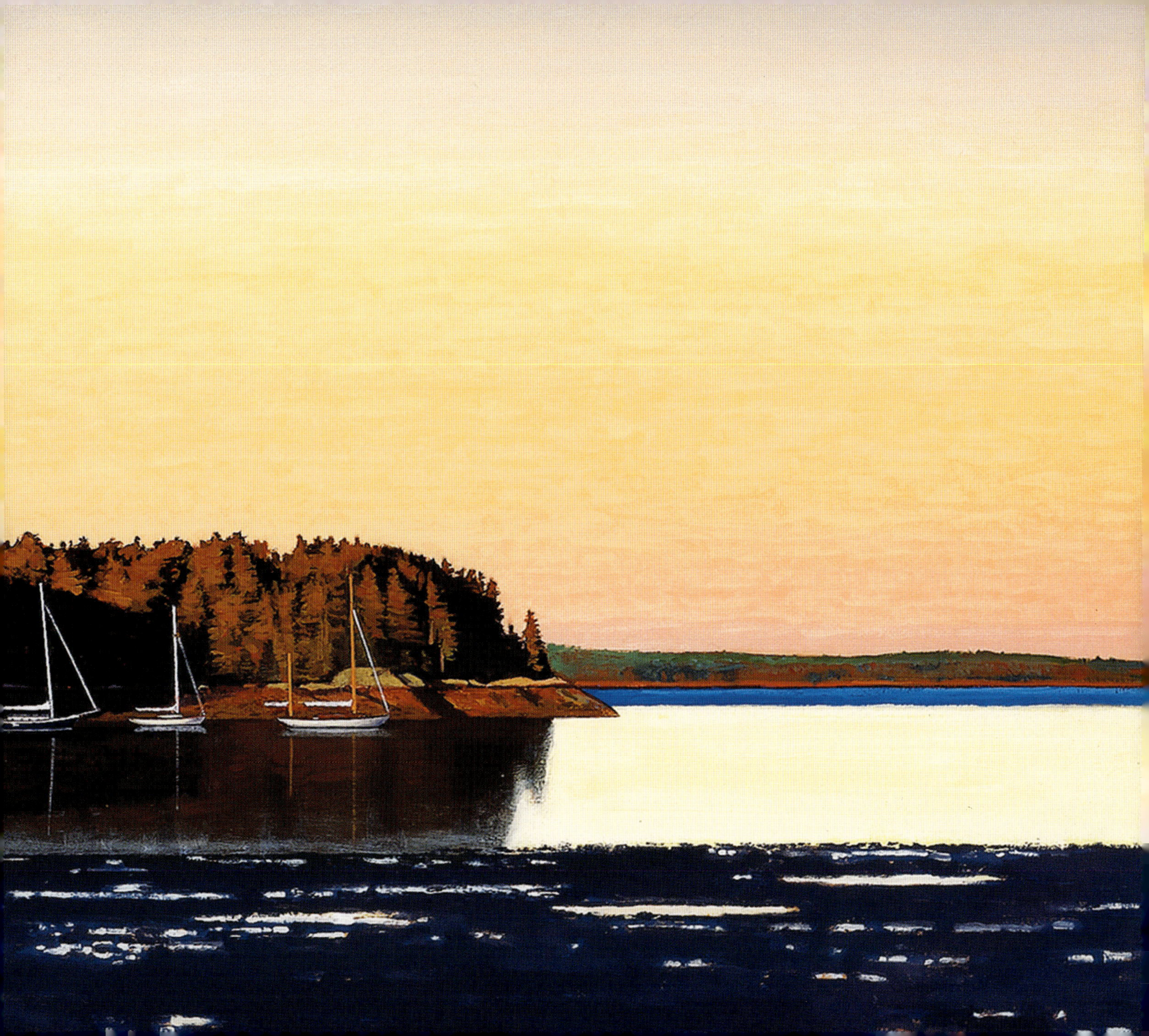

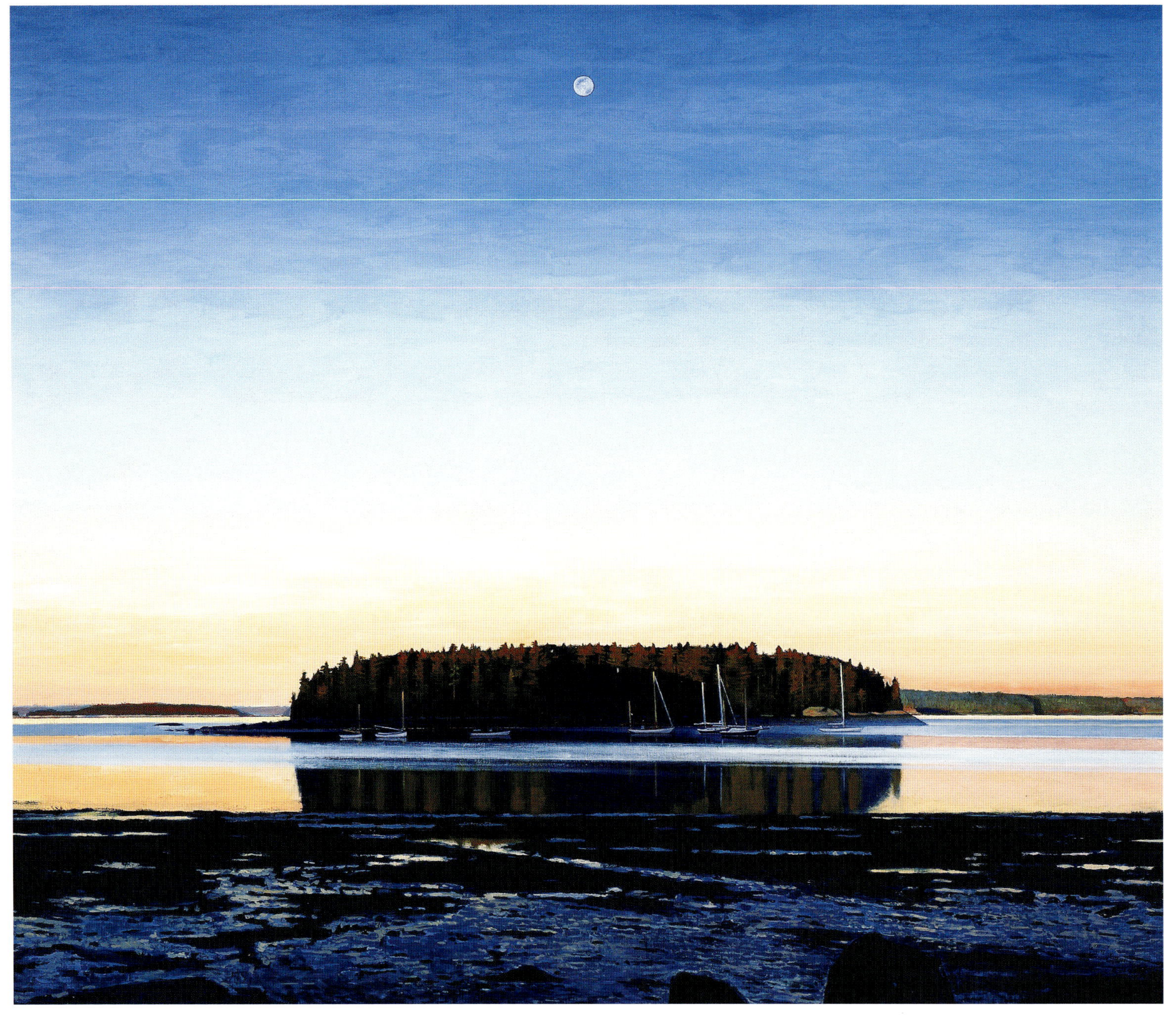

Moon Over Harbor, oil on panel, 36" x 43", private collection.

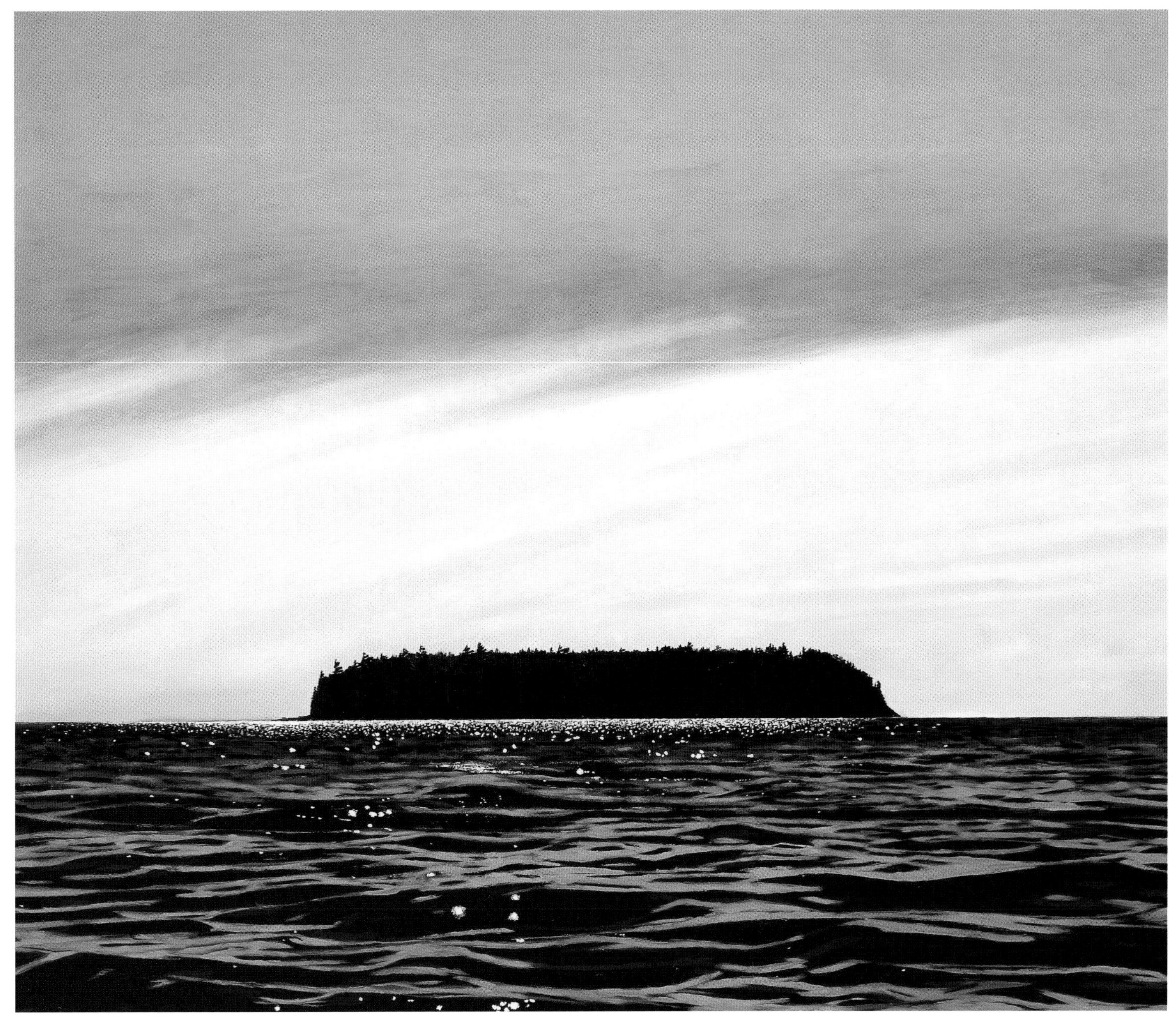

Shimmer, oil on panel, 48" x 57", collection of Matt and Ann Adriance.

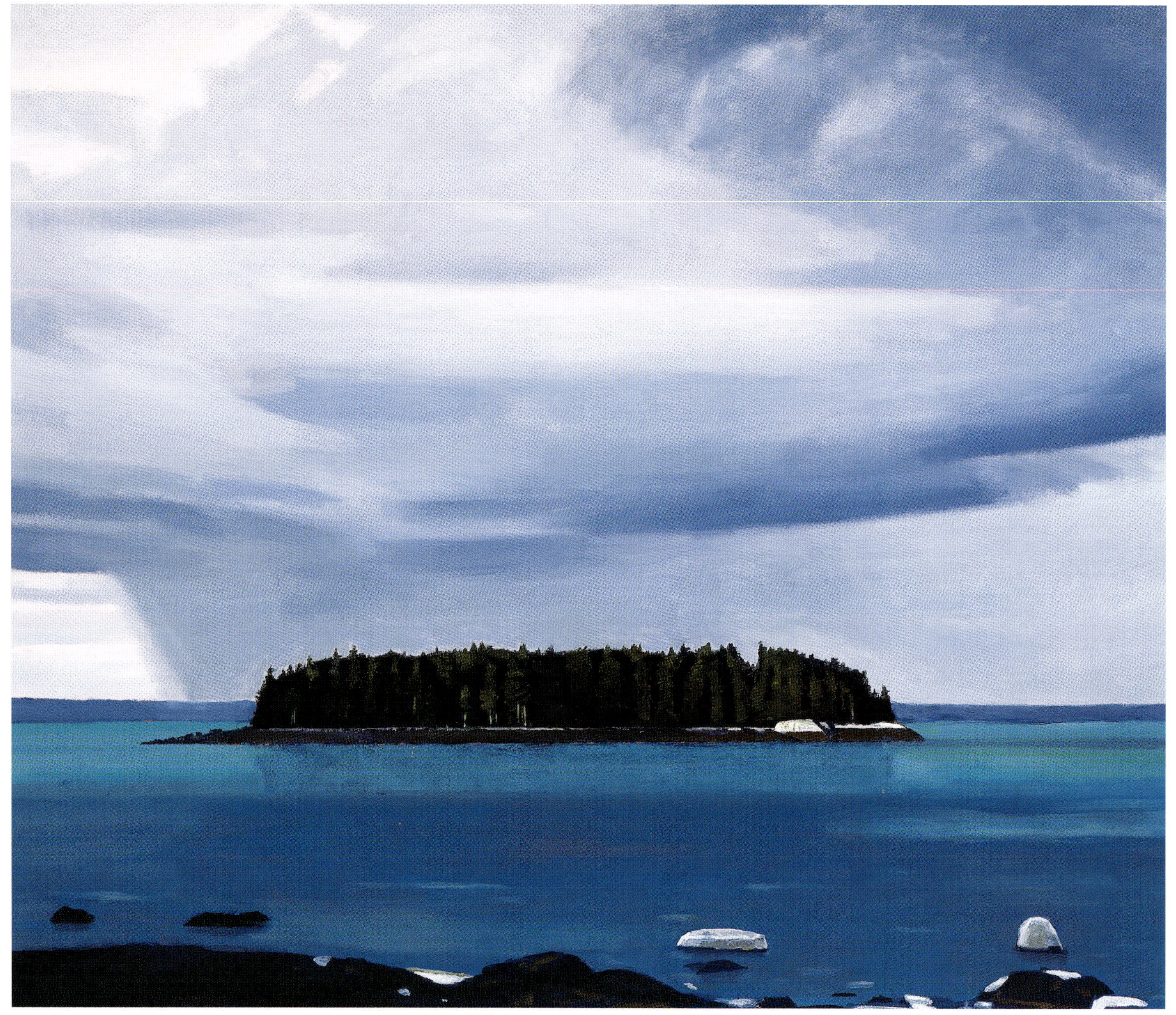

Thunderstorm, oil on panel, 36" x 43", collection of the artist.

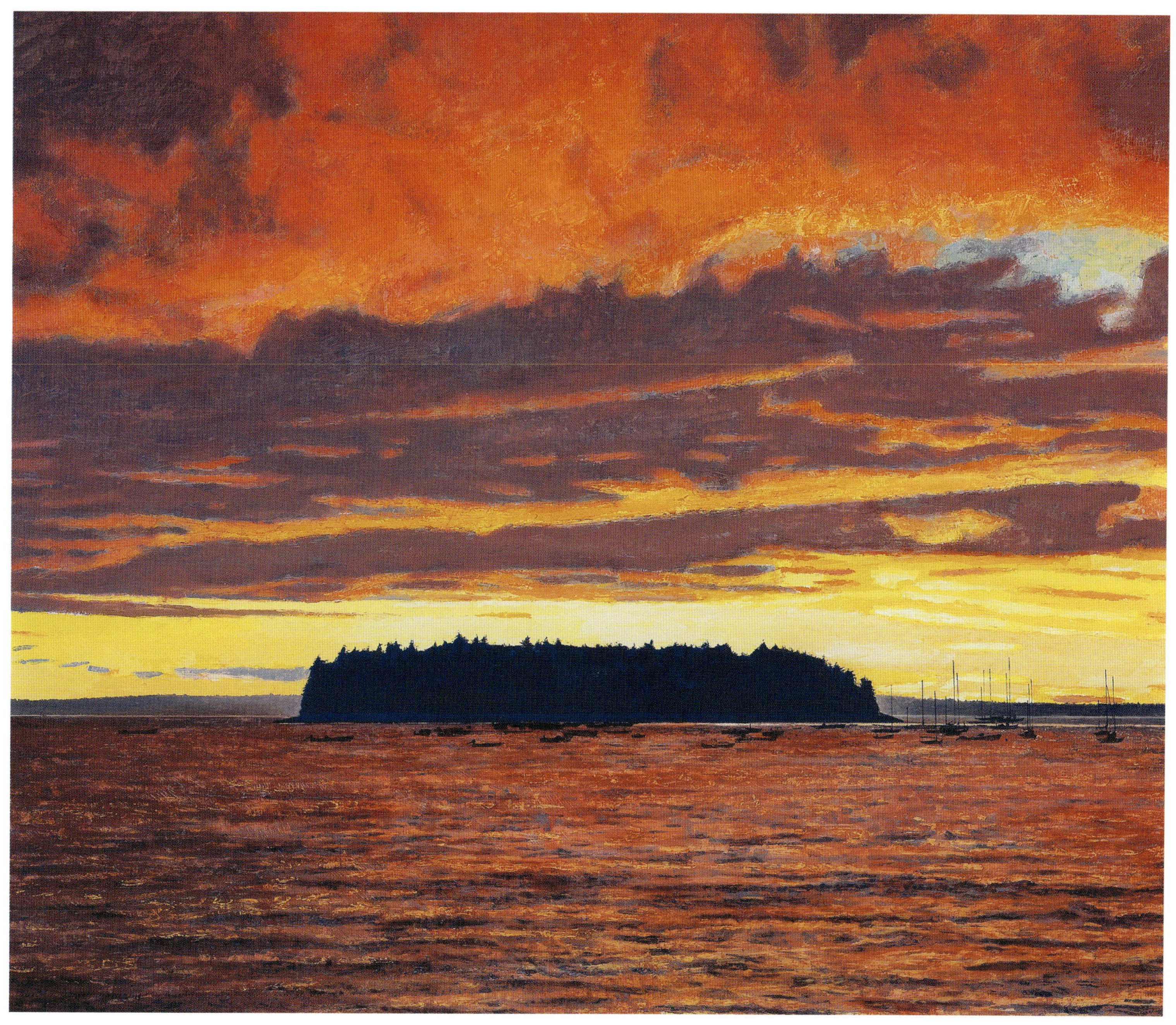

Red Sky, oil on panel, 48" x 57", collection of Nancy and Bucky Kales.

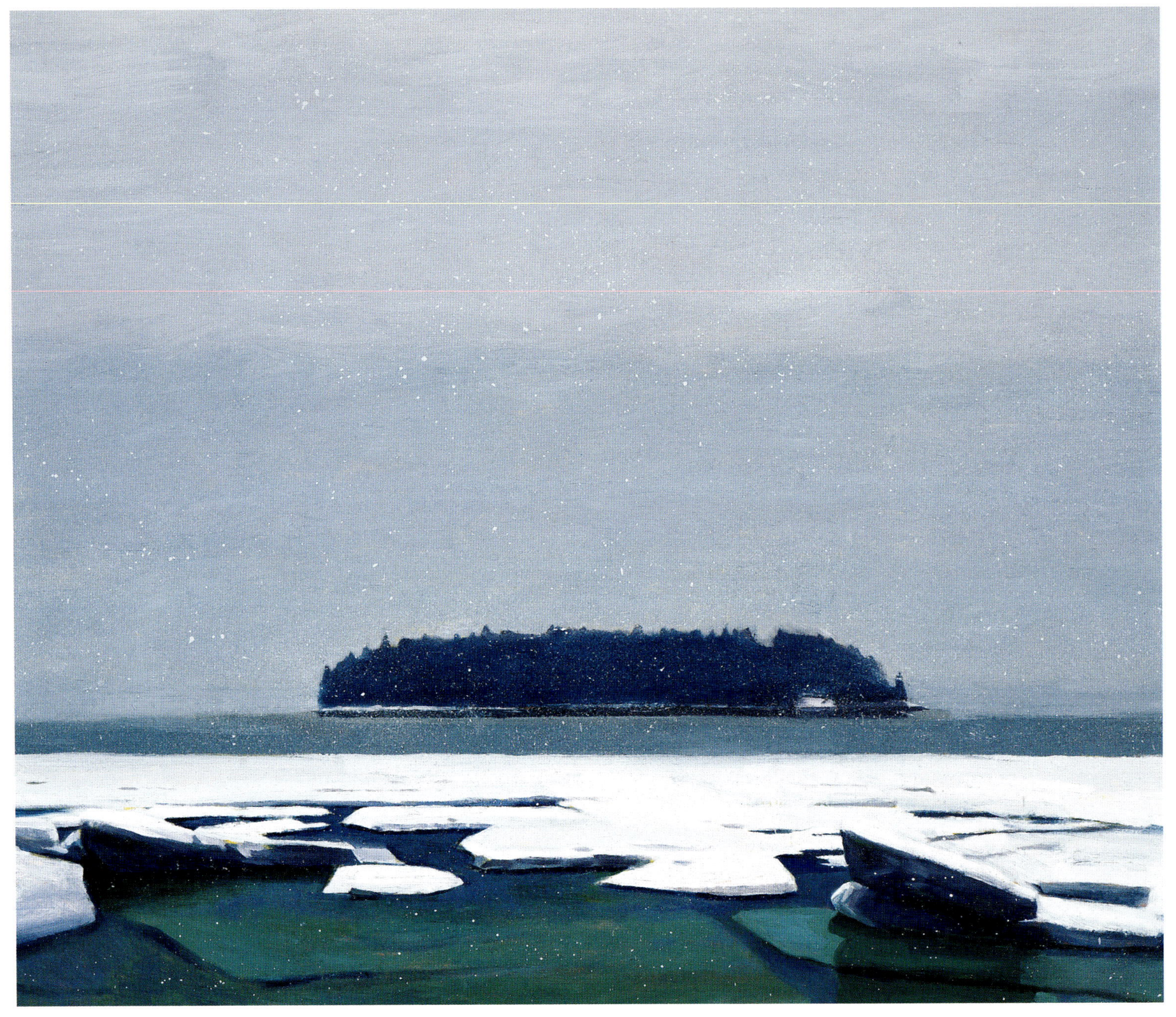

January Thaw, oil on panel, 36" x 43", collection of Patrick Wilmerding.

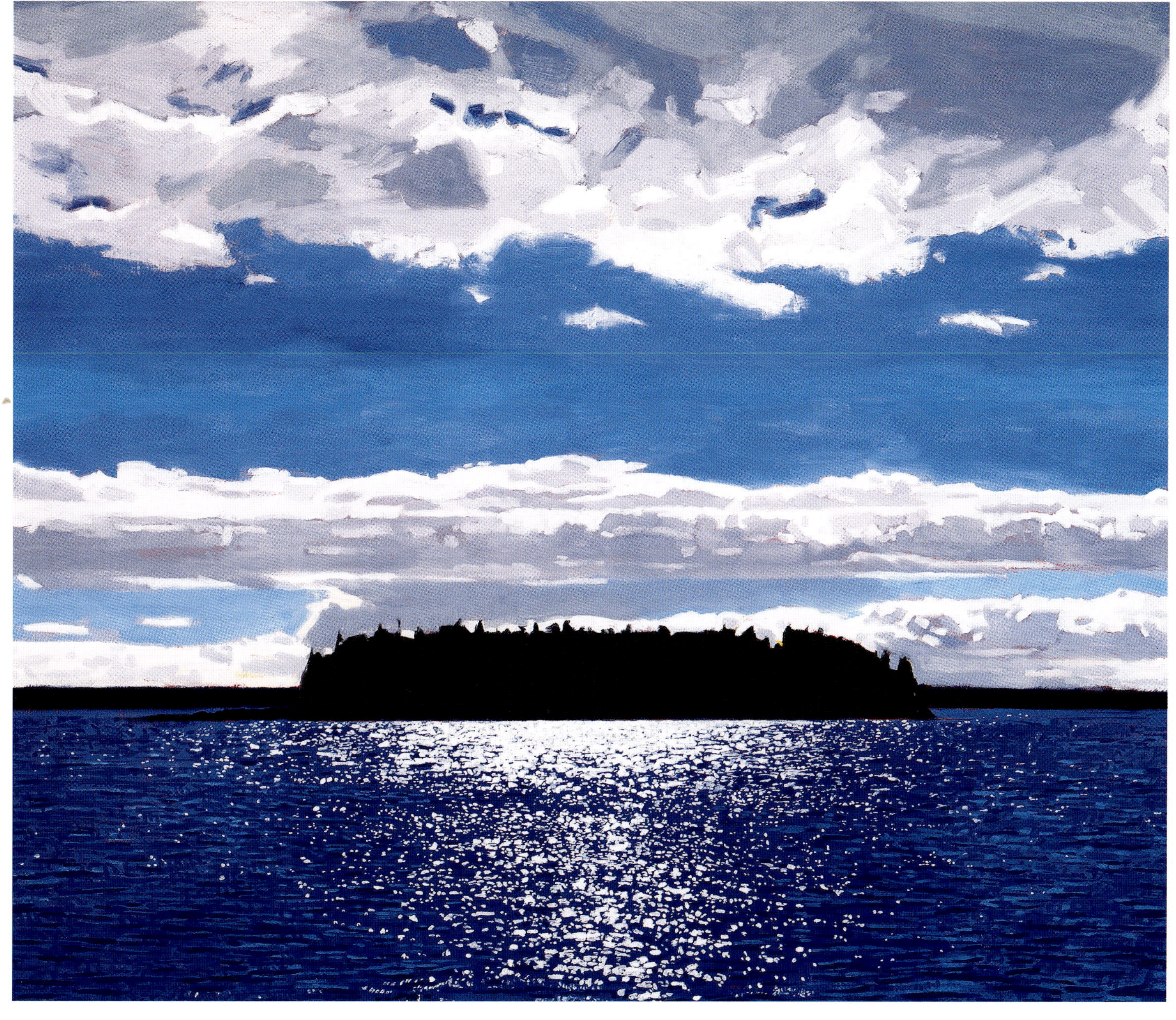

Equinox, oil on panel, 48" x 57", collection of Ken Moller.

overleaf: *January Thaw,* oil on panel, 36" x 43", collection of Patrick Wilmerding.

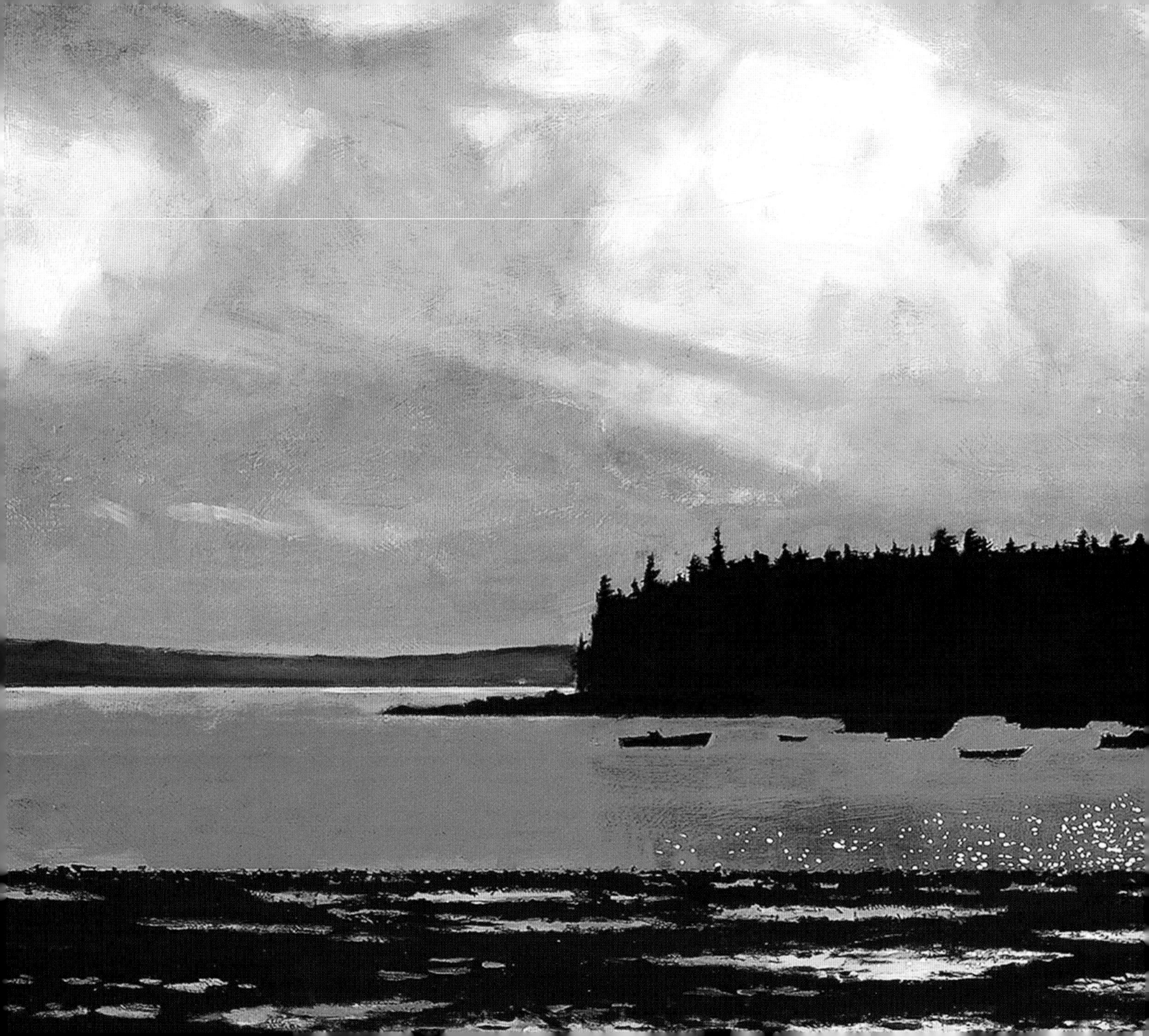

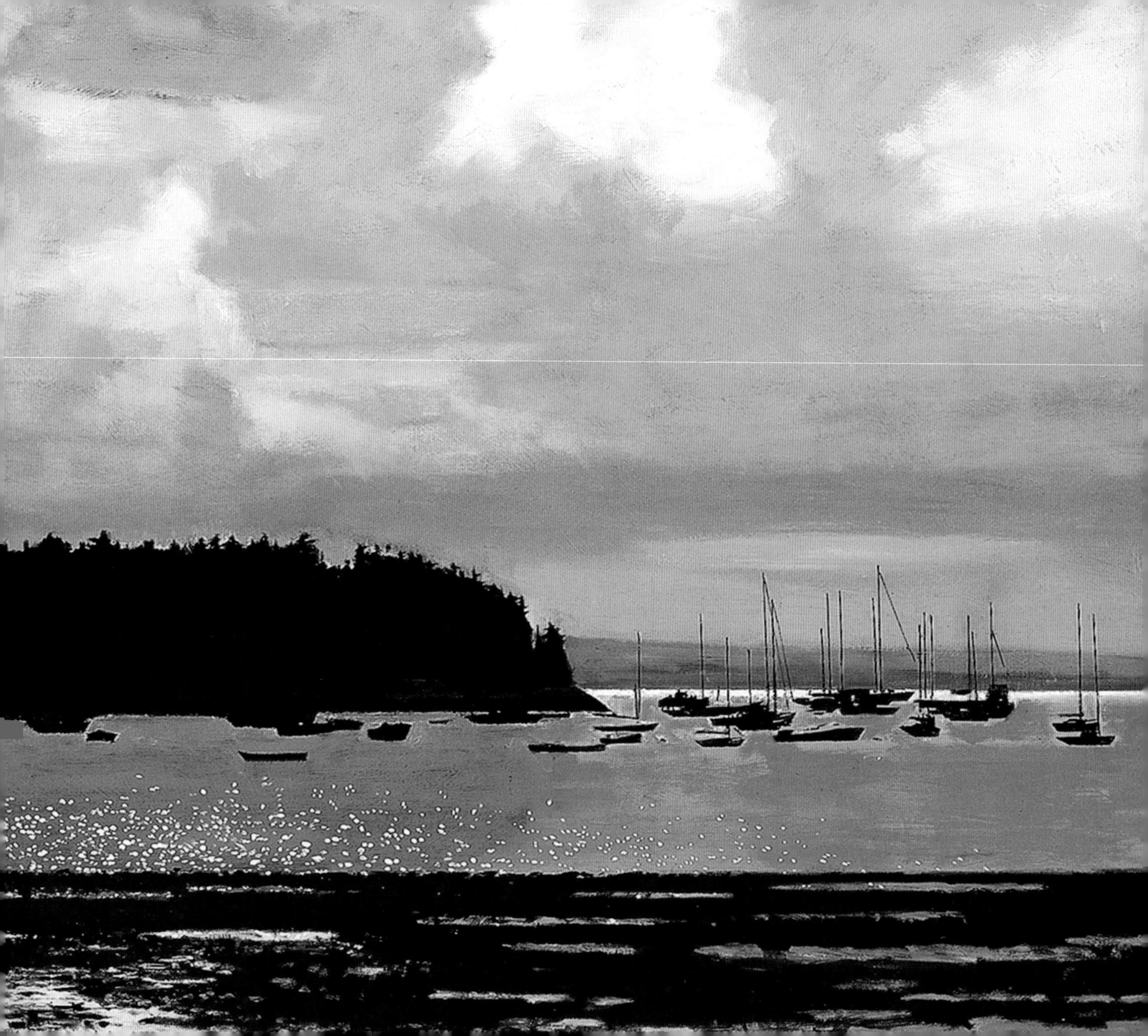

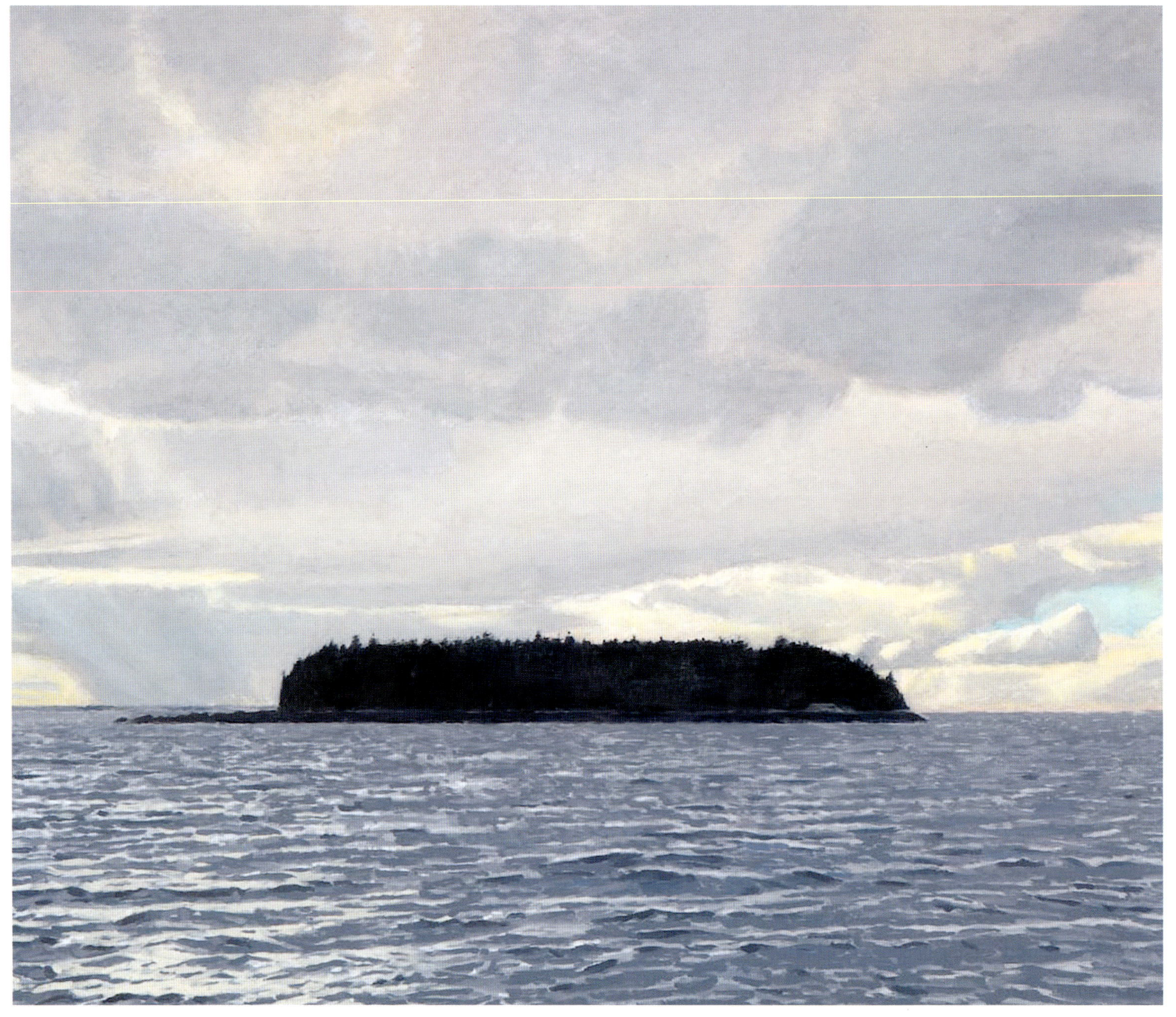

Southerly, oil on panel, 36" x 43", collection of the artist.

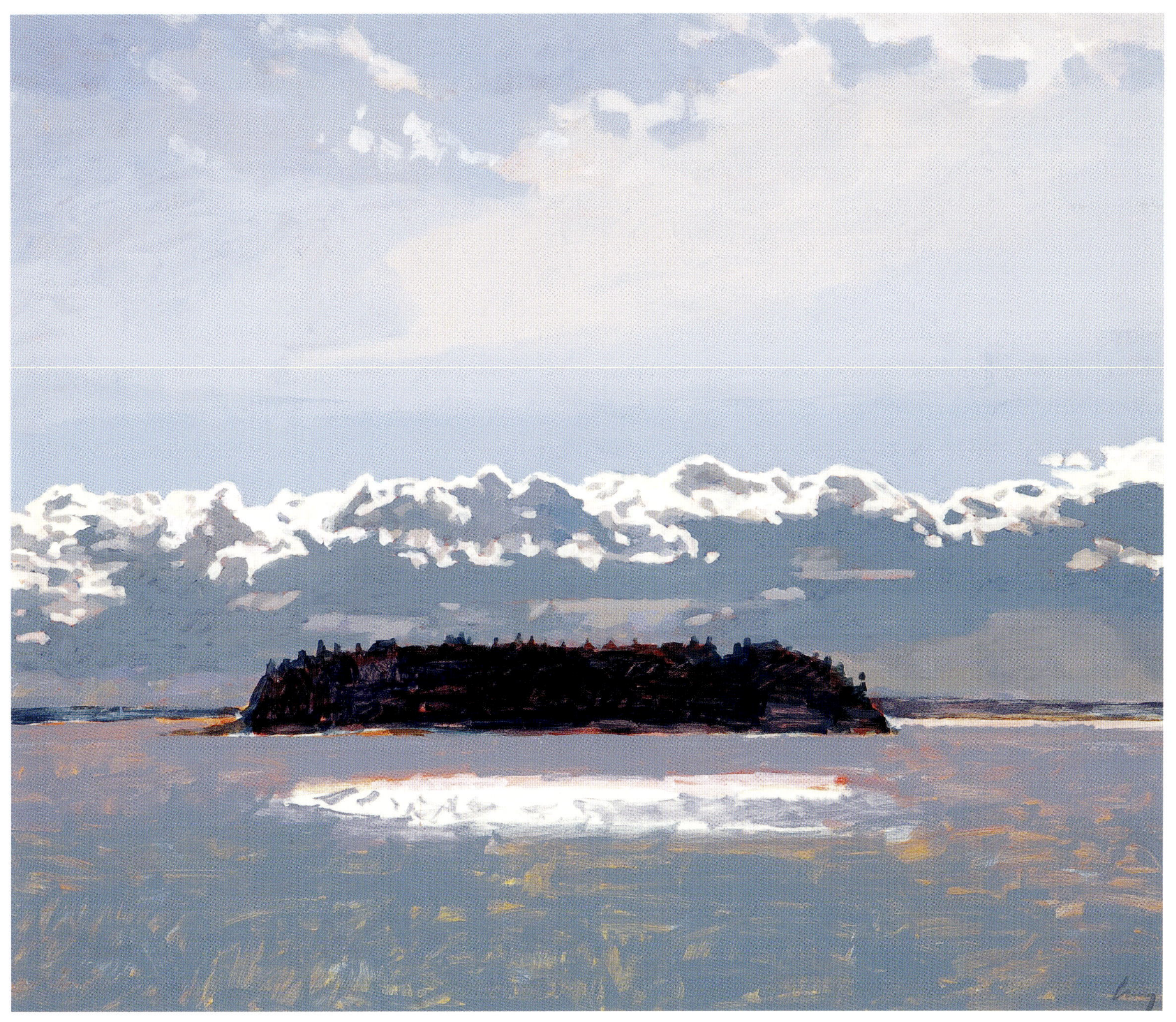

Cloud Bank, acrylic on panel, 36" x 43", collection of the artist.

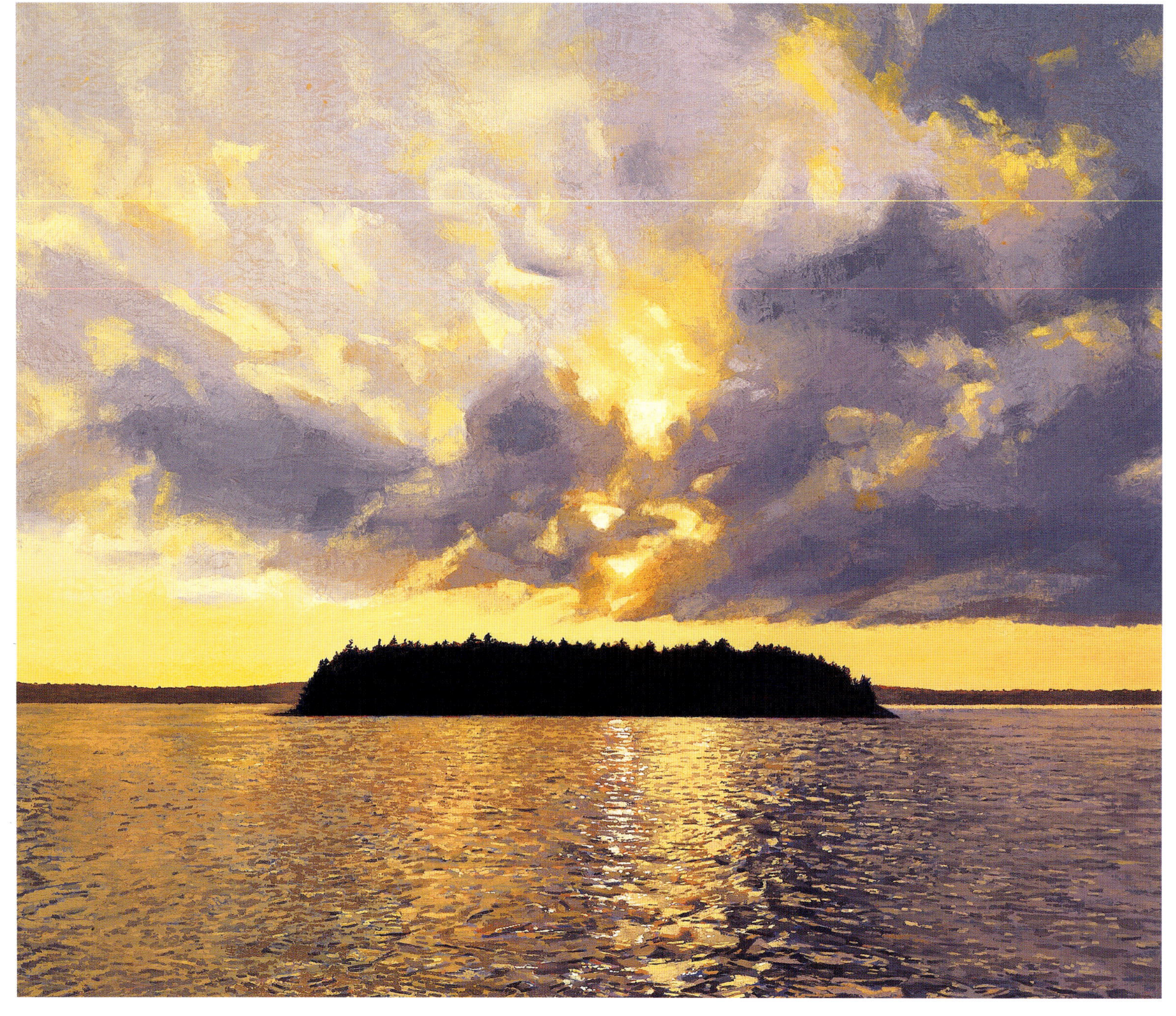

Il Tramonto, oil on panel, 48" x 57", collection of C. David O'Brien.

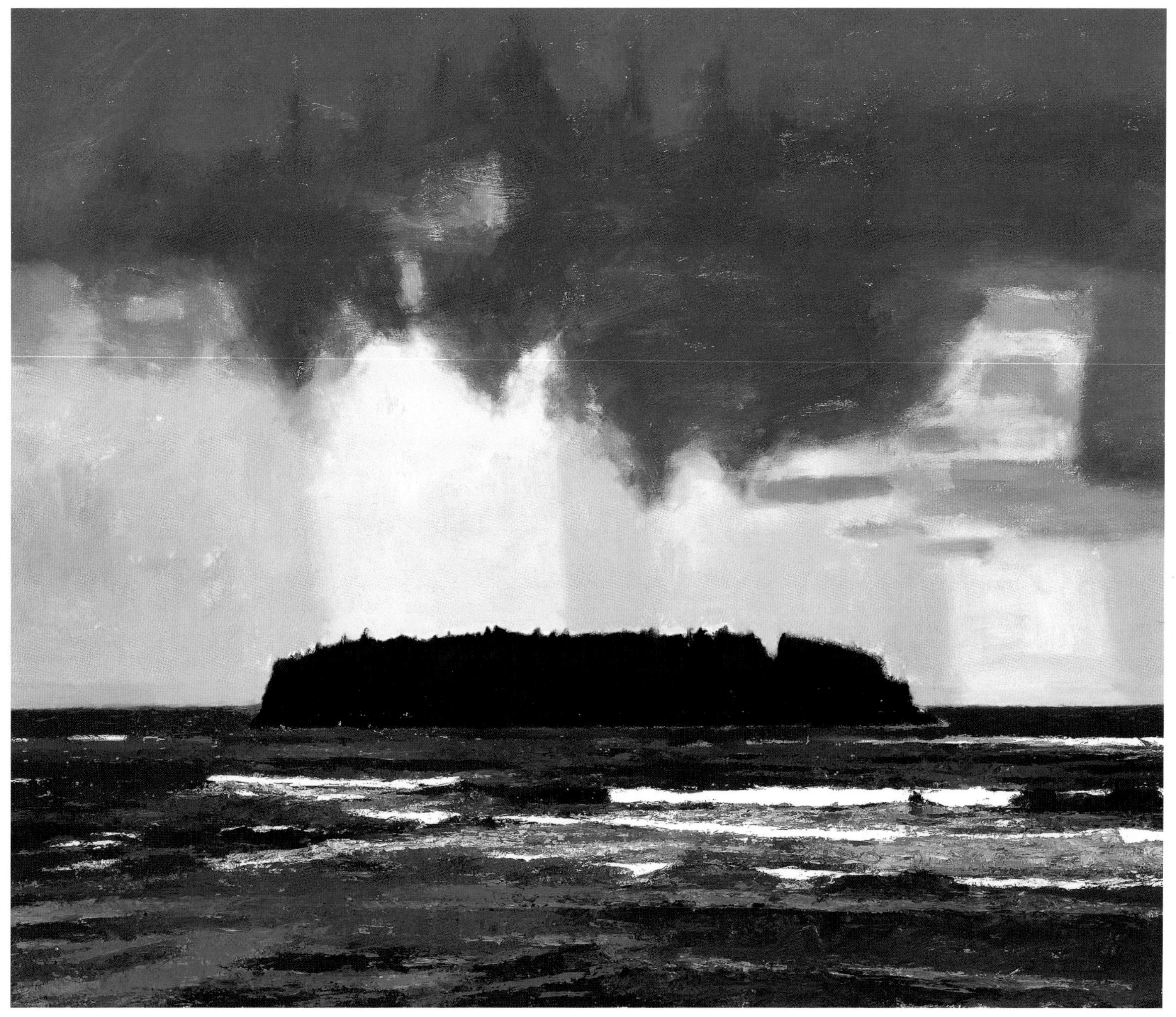

Line Squall, oil on panel, 36" x 43", collection of the artist.

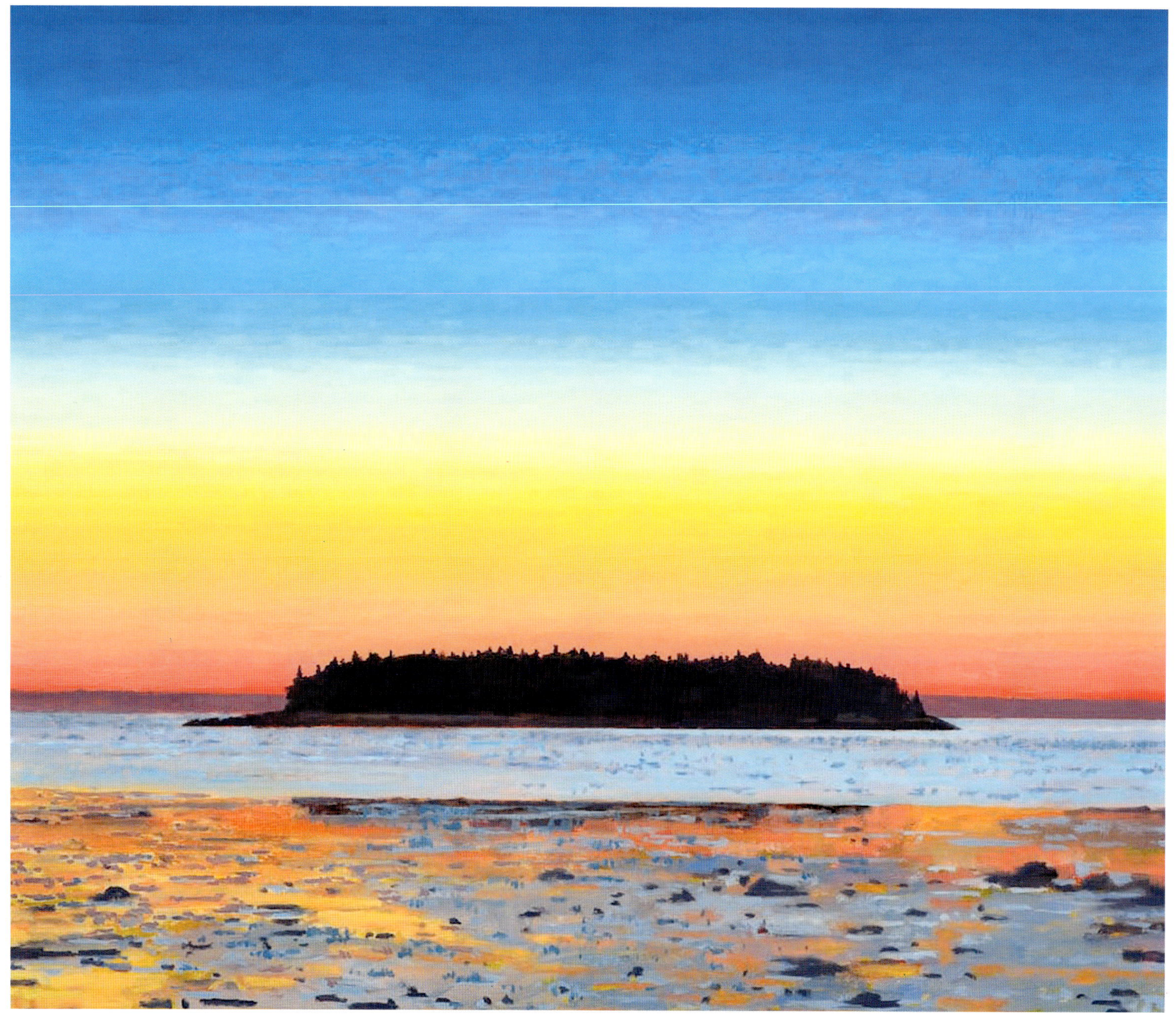

Glow, oil on panel, 36" x 43", collection of the artist.

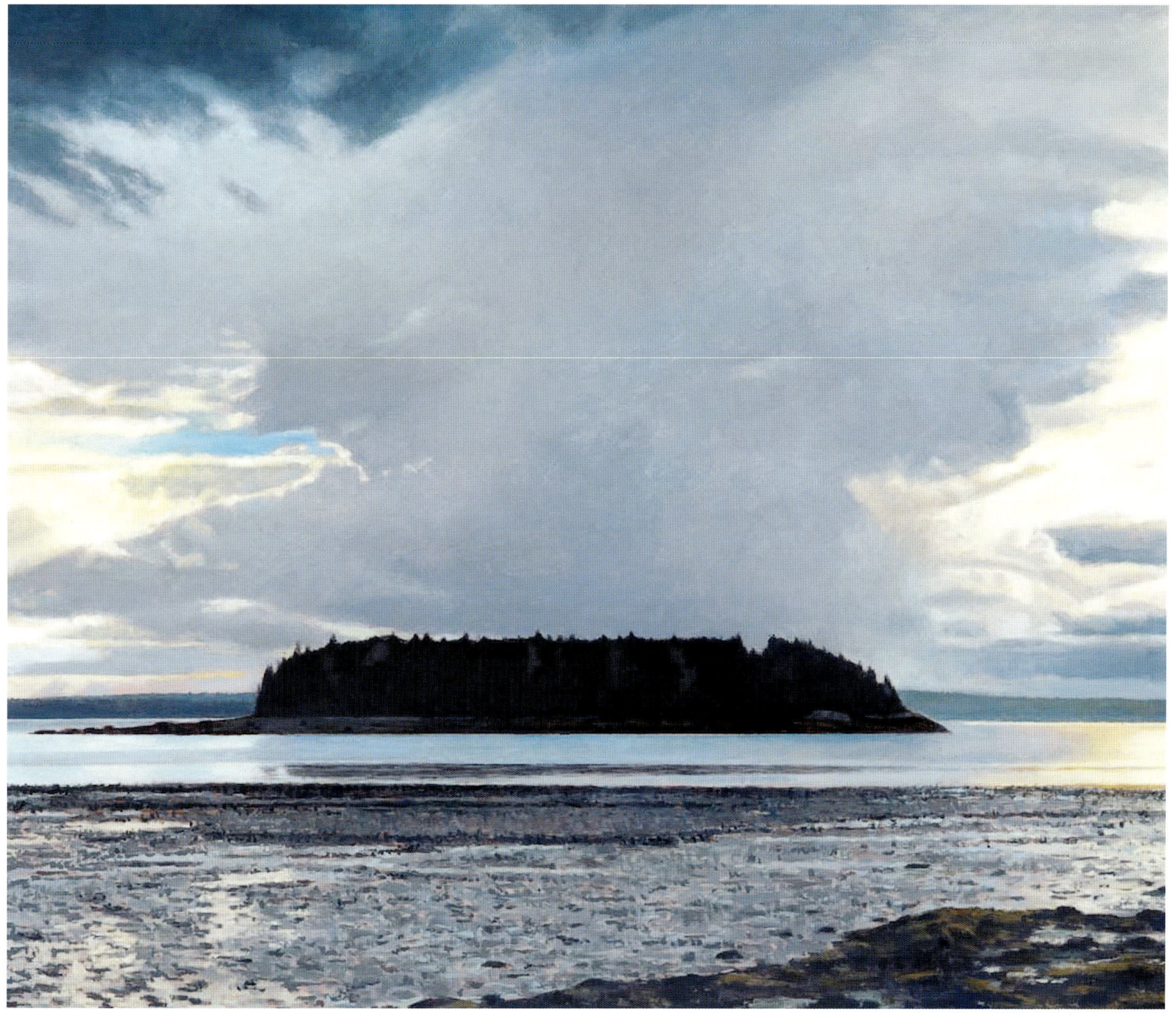

Spring Storm, oil on panel, 36" x 43", Mark Tucker collection.

overleaf: *Approaching Storm,* oil on panel, 48" x 57", collection of the artist.

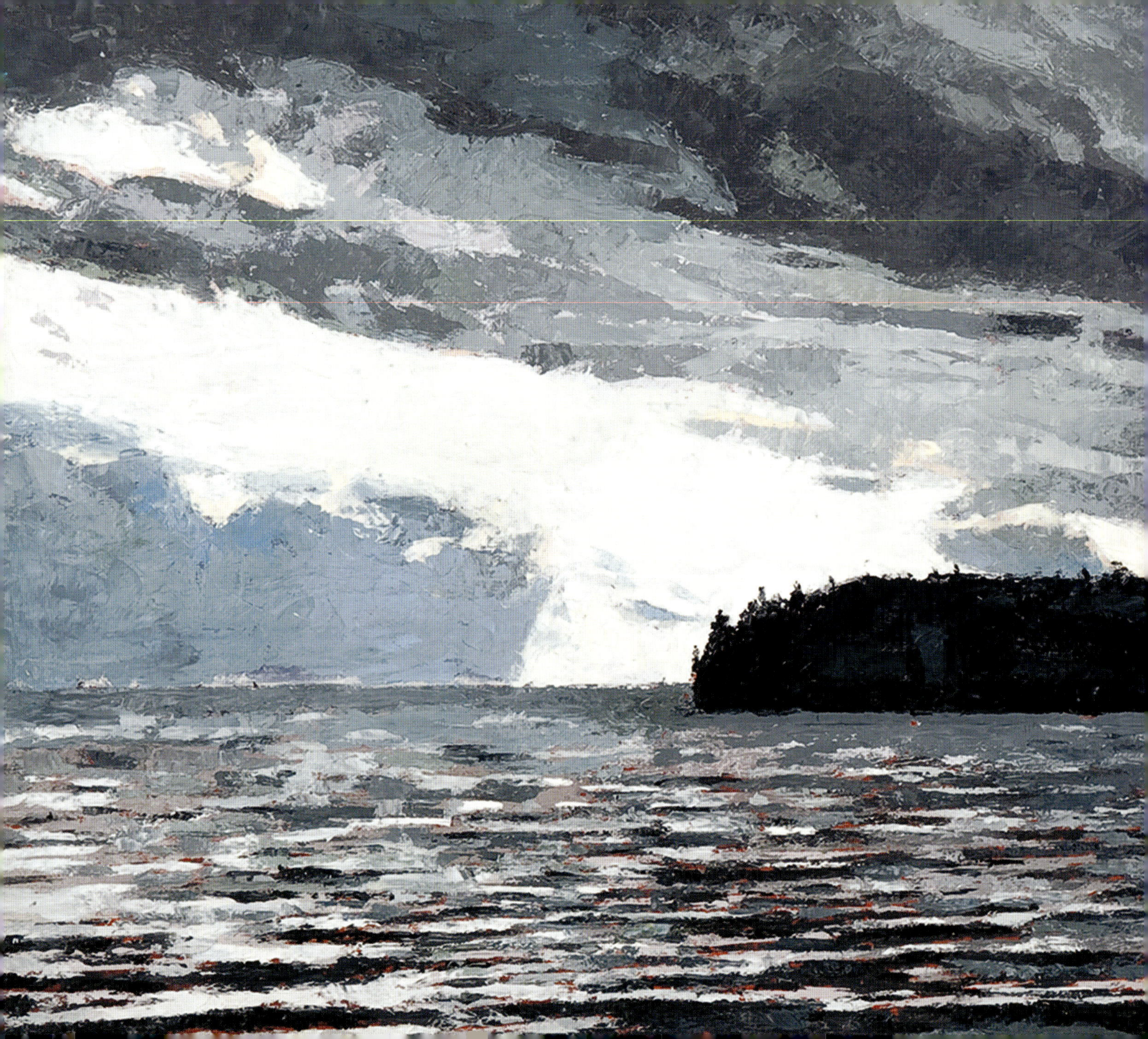

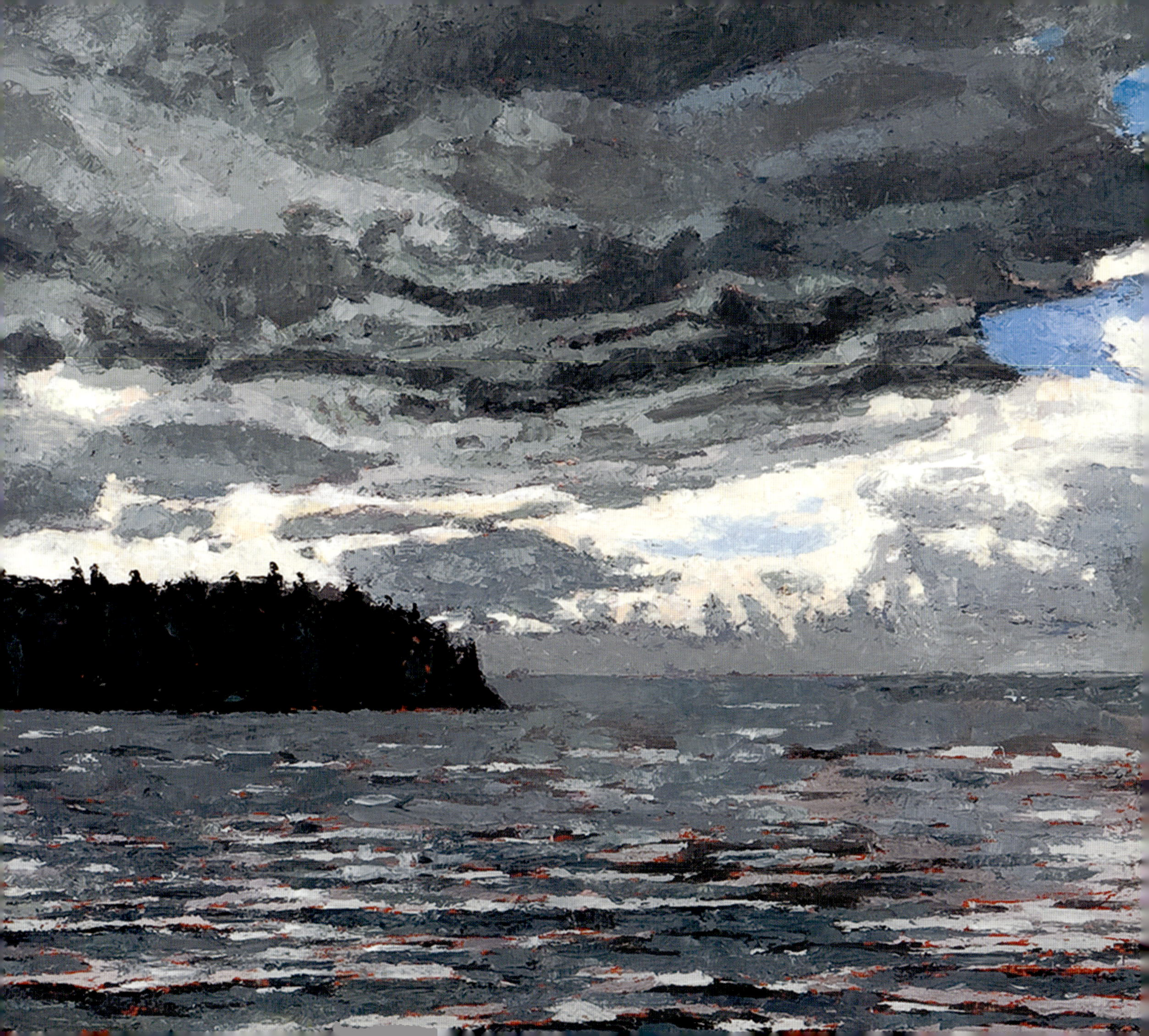

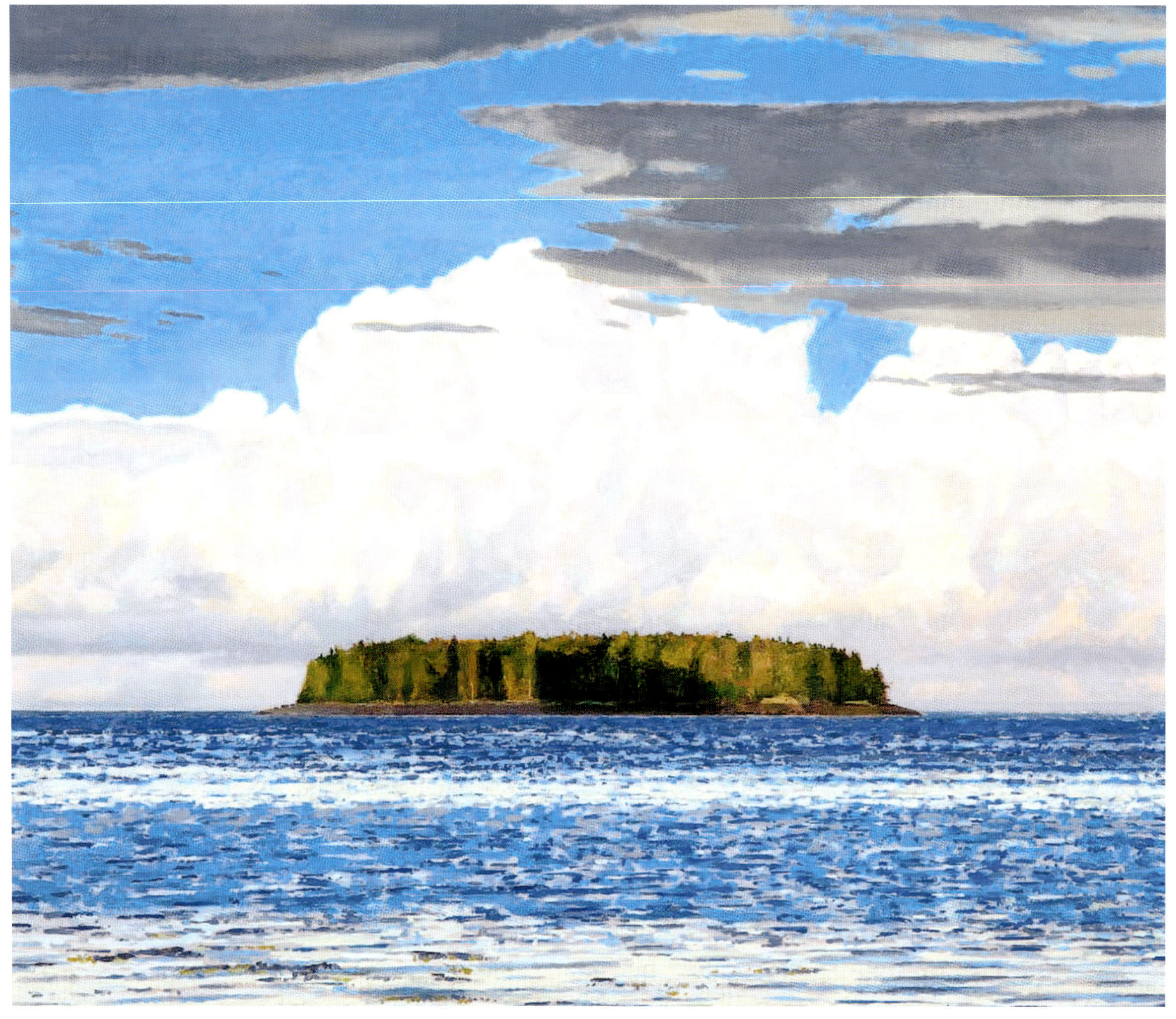

Thunderheads, oil on panel, 36" x 43", collection of the artist.

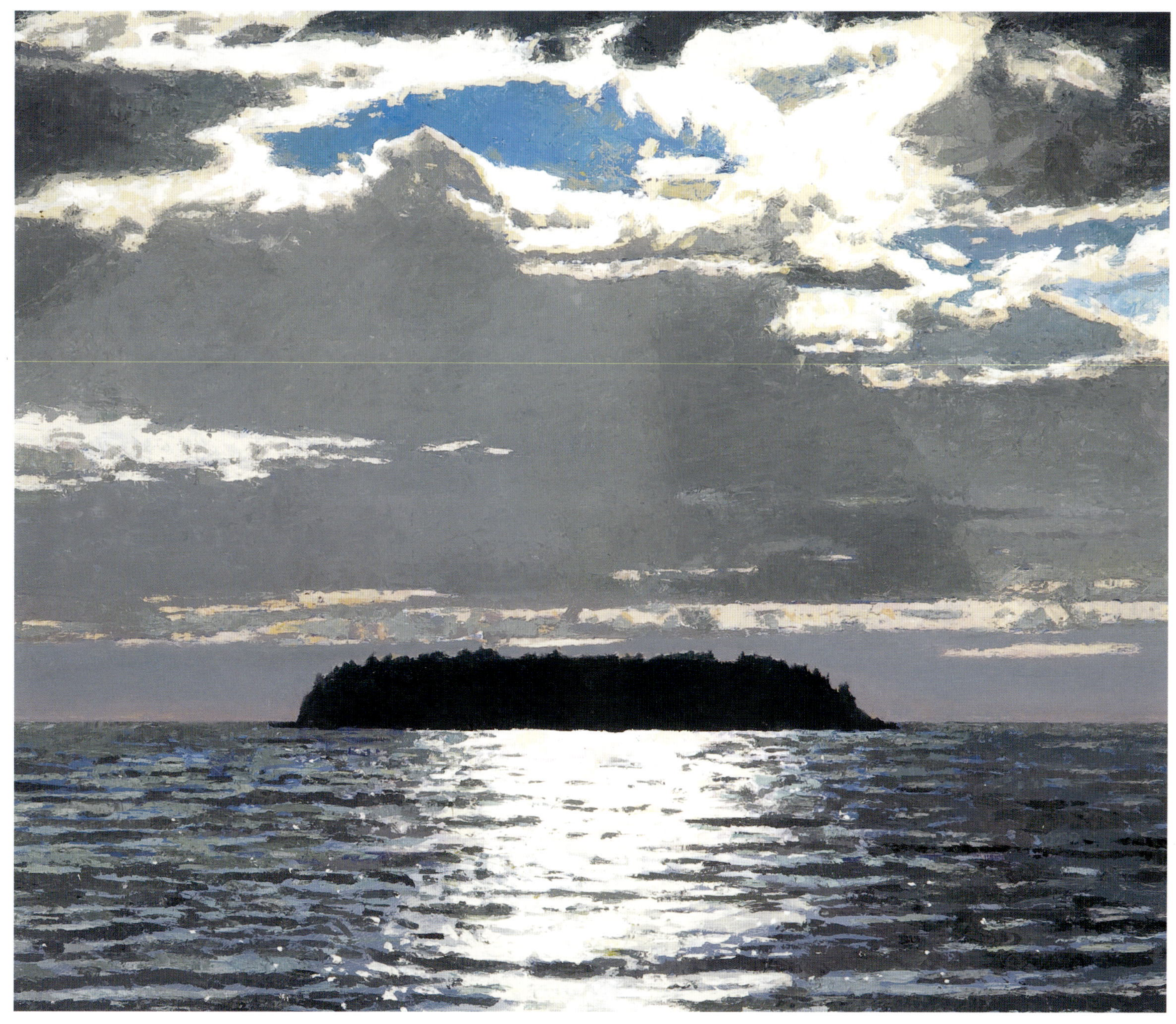

Glimpse of Blue, oil on panel, 48" x 57", collection of the artist.

"The moments when the mind is absorbed by beauty are the only hours when we really live. All else is illusion or mere endurance."

—Richard Jeffries

Clearing, oil on panel, 36" x 43", collection of Nancy and Bucky Kales.

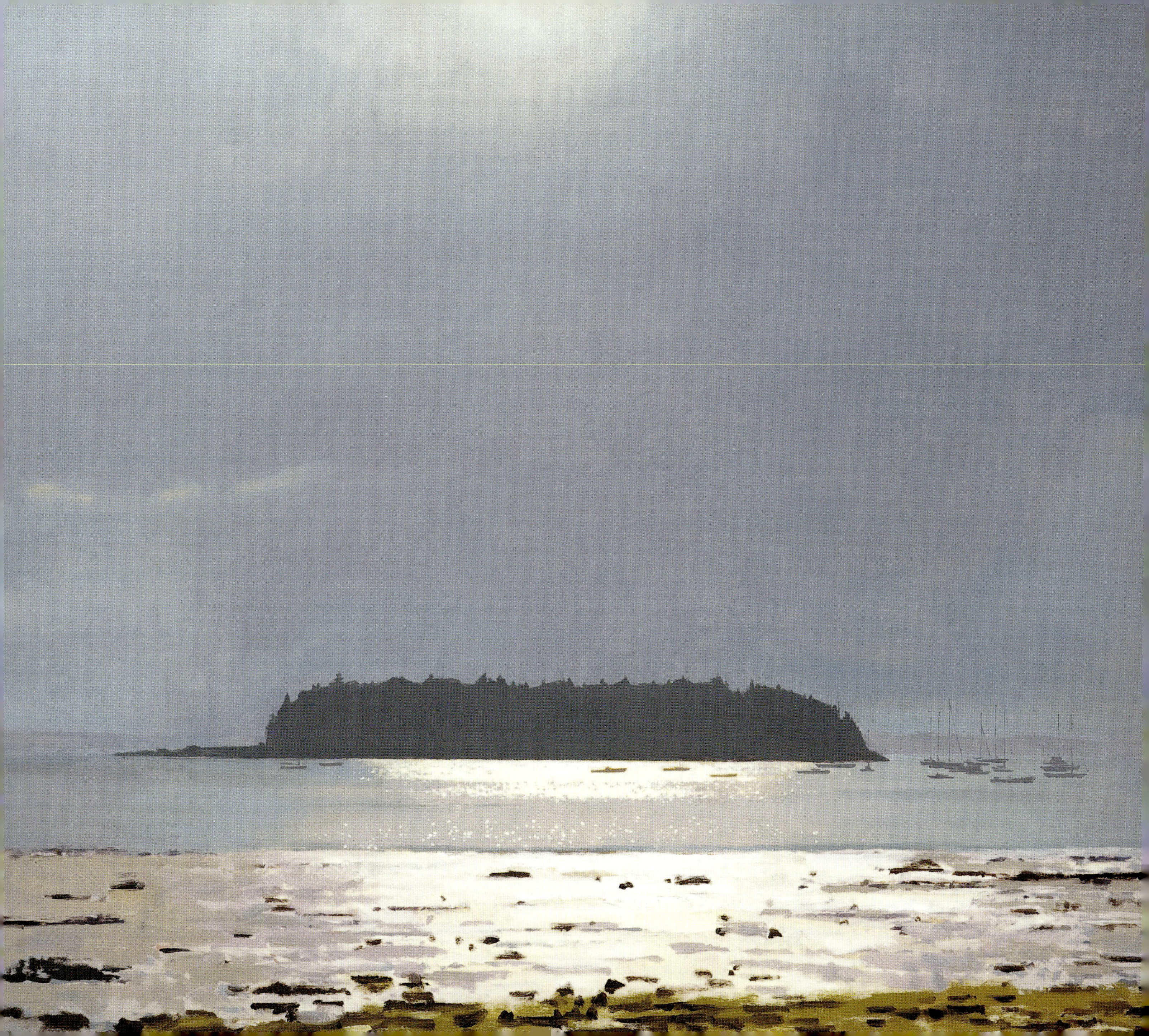

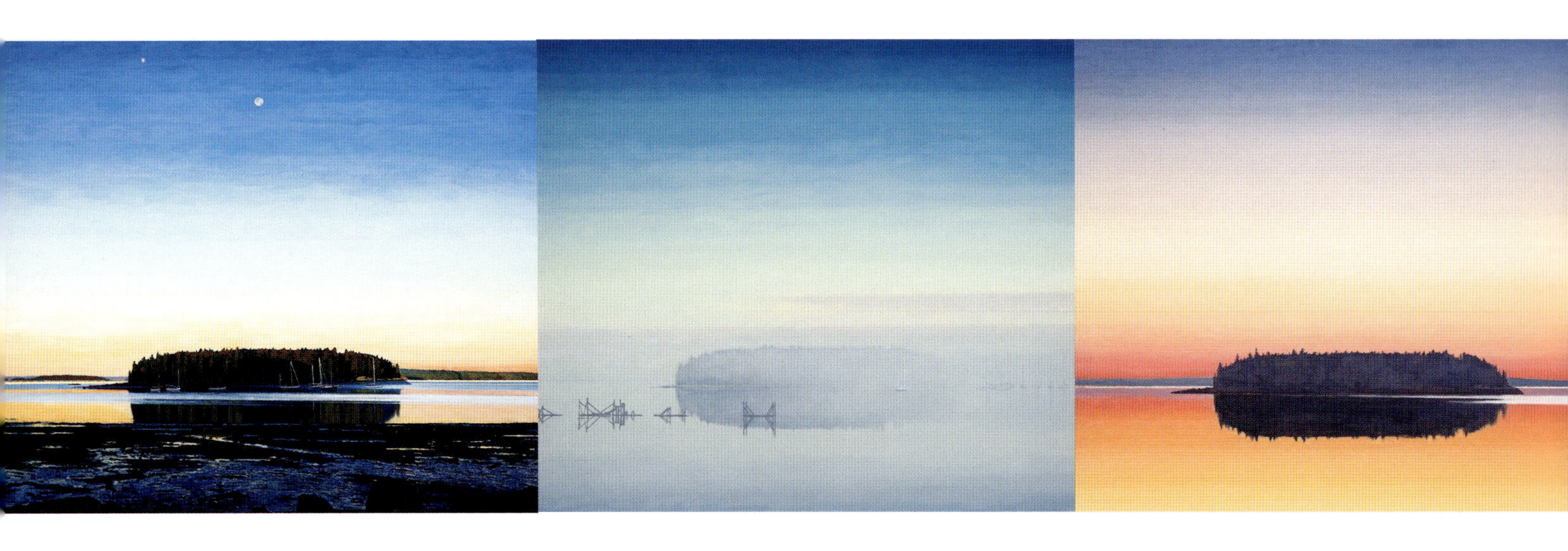

Acknowledgements

More people than I can name have inspired and encouraged me to do the work I love. Thanks to my parents, Bob and Carol Curry; Nancy and Bucky Kales for inspiration; Terry Tempest Williams for her eloquent questions; Jan Cigliano Hartman for being a catalyst; William Braden for introducing me to landscape painting; a wide community of friends and brilliant painters here in Maine; extraordinary teachers at RISD, including Lorraine Shemesh, Panos Ghikas, and the late George Pappas and Francis Harpin. Finally, to my wife Kimberly for believing in me.

overleaf: *Tempest,* oil on panel, 36" x 43", collection of Nancy and Bucky Kales.

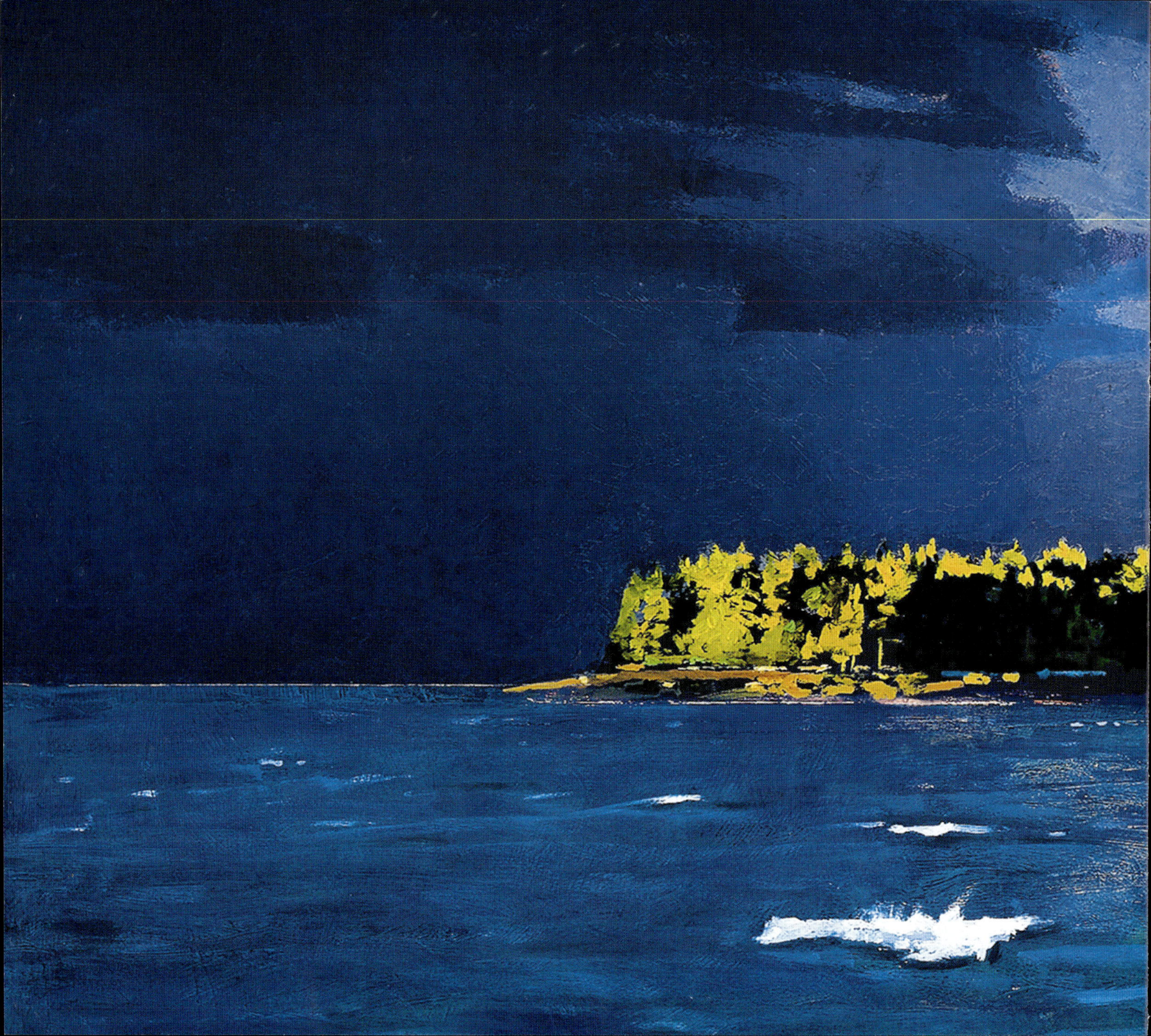

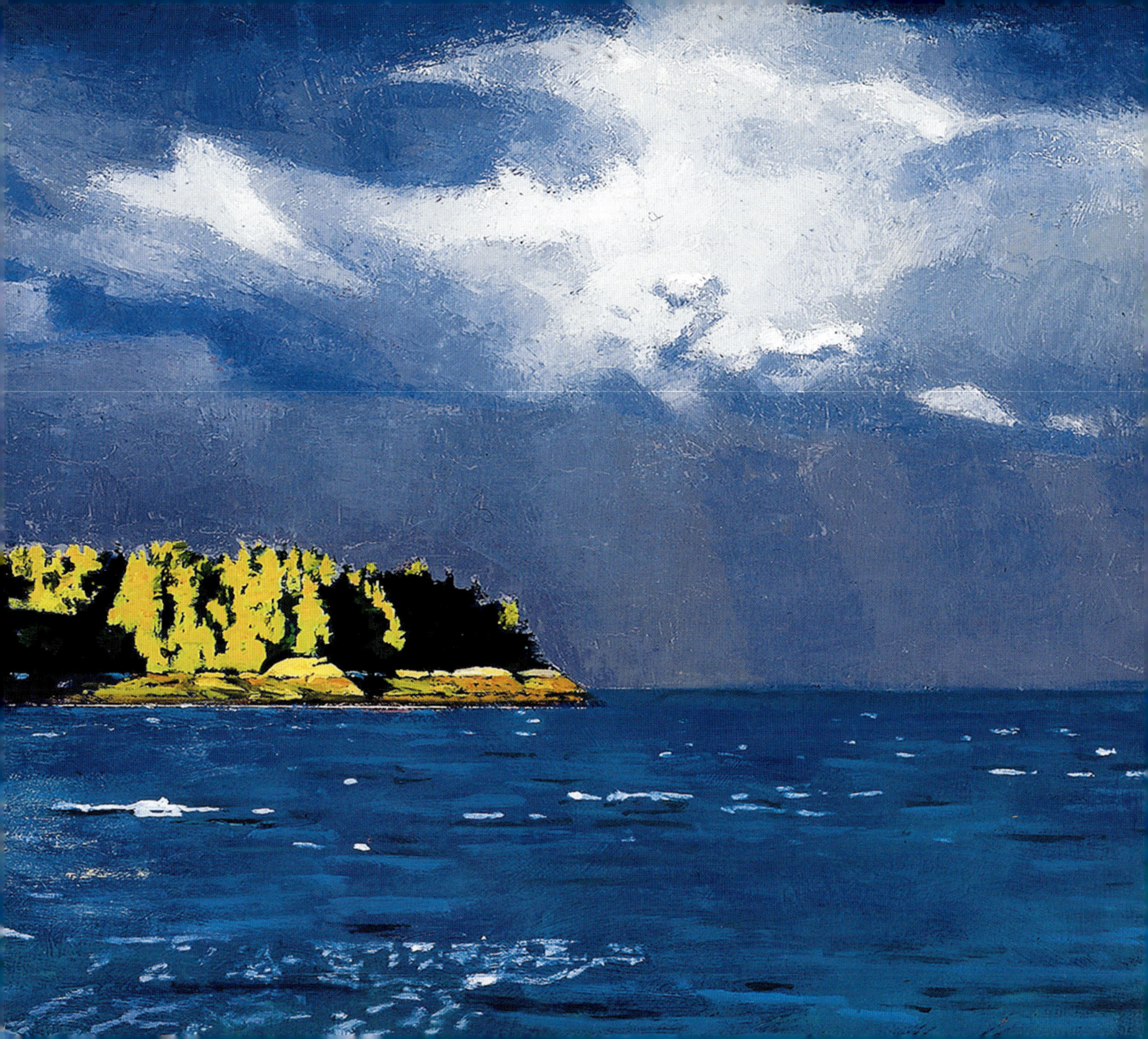